WHITE COLLAR WITCH HUNT

The
Catholic Priesthood
Under Siege

William L. Roth, Jr.
Foreword by Timothy Parsons-Heather

The Morning Star of Our Lord, Inc. is a nonprofit, tax-exempt, 501(c)(3), religious and charitable organization which is incorporated under the Laws of the State of Illinois. It has been established for the dissemination of various apologetic works in defense of the Truth of the Holy Gospel of Christianity. It is the intrinsic role of this Corporation to provide pastoral consolation to those lacking in faith, the infirm, homebound, incarcerated, deprived, dejected, and those who are otherwise suffering humanity for the sake of the Glory of the Kingdom of Jesus Christ. All proceeds from this book are being donated to other charitable causes to help feed, clothe, and house the poor, and for the reproduction of this spiritual manuscript for distribution on every continent of the world. If anyone would like to contribute to this worthy cause, you may do so through the following postal and website addresses.

The Morning Star of Our Lord, Inc.
Post Office Box 8584
Springfield, Illinois 62791-8584
www.ImmaculateMary.org

ISBN: 0-9671587-3-7

Printed in the United States of America

White Collar Witch Hunt
The Catholic Priesthood Under Siege

Table of Contents

Section One
Robed in Majesty

Section Two
The Monopoly of Truth

Section Three
Go Make of All Disciples

Commemorations

Dedication
to the
Light of Divine Truth

For the dignity of humankind, the sanctification of the soul, the inspiration of the heart, and the confirming of our Salvation in the Blood of Jesus Christ, we must invoke, emit, respect, and dispense the timeless Love of God through every generation; past, present, and future; that our spiritual holiness will forever become a consolation to the community of nations, a beacon to those lost in the darkness of their sins, the splendor of Christian revelation to the many who are hidden beneath the burdens of prejudice; goodness, joy, and harmony to the prosecutors and victims of worlds at war, and the exaltation of moral genius to the lost who are still searching for the meaning of human life. We hold to the fashioned excellence that Our Lord is the Convener of Life, our Sustainer, our Pardoner, and our Judge; and that it is only through His Holy Grace that we shall live again. Linear time is much like a fuse leading to a giant firecracker that, when lit by the Flame of Truth, will come back and blow our errant past into Kingdom Come someday. To the hopes of millions, their devoted progeny, the parameters of ecclesiastical Wisdom, the fairness of the intellect, the chastity of the flesh, and the legacy of our compliance with the transcendent Mysteries of the Crucifixion of Jesus Christ, I dedicate this book to the Light of Divine Truth by which we are led in faith; healed by His Martyrdom, emboldened by the Holy Paraclete, disciplined through the intercession of the Most Blessed Virgin Mary, and raised into the jubilation of immortality in the unfolding Triumph of Her Immaculate Heart of Love.

-William L. Roth, Jr.

Mortal sin is a radical possibility of human freedom, as is Love, itself. It results in the loss of charity and the privation of sanctifying grace, that is, of the state of grace. If it is not redeemed by repentance and God's forgiveness, it causes exclusion from Christ's Kingdom and the eternal death of Hell; for our freedom has the power to make choices forever, with no turning back. However, although we can judge that an act is, in itself, a grave offense, we must entrust judgement of persons to the justice and Mercy of God.

Catechism of the Roman Catholic Church
Part Three, Section I, Article 8, 1861

Foreword

While there is no doubt that all things shall be revealed in time, it often seems as though the clock somehow stops during the interim and our anticipation becomes trite and log-jammed while we endure the wait. The immediacy of our fallible human judgement, however, seems to prevail over the fullness of the facts and the more logical aspects about the process of how we render our decisions when approaching daily life. Humanity should remember that we are all sinners in the flesh and that our very creation is a function of the loyalty of God to His Own Eternal Will; the same Almighty Being who is presently attempting to effect the perfection of our souls, despite the countless ways we try to deny Him by unwittingly sauntering down some other path. There can be no doubt that His agenda has always revolved around making the universes one mass of unified spiritual matter inside the Sacred Heart of Jesus before the end of time arrives. The longstanding argument as to whether we can actually recapture our human innocence before we die still resides at the fore of our discussion; and those who proclaim that we will always be corrupt because we have a propensity to transgress have already given-up the fight. They tend to forget that our Christian Baptism is the lifting of our souls beyond the threshold of original sin, into the new life of absolution we have gained in the Crucifixion of Our Lord. And, just as Christ has shown us, there is nothing even slightly symbolic in this; but rather a real, true, functional, and retrievable grace from the Throne of Love into the everyday world. When God's hands were itching in expectation that His people would soon be coming home aboard the Palms of the Messiah as the first century slowly unfolded, it was *humanity* who drove steel spikes into them instead; proclaiming in staunch arrogance that we could find another fare. We are the haughty ones who have declined His invitation to be consistent in the dispensing of our will by praising and petting only our wares and riches, the contours of our flesh, and the succulent lambs we have cooked to perfection over the coals of our crimson dinner flames. What is it that makes humankind believe that all command, divine power, and our state of endless "being" must somehow be a product of our own discrimination; placing our emphasis in some fulsome itinerary that takes us only into the mazes where our ancestors have previously withered?

The fact remains true that we are responsible to assist one another in becoming the likeness of Christ only after we have embarked upon this same journey, ourselves. No mortal man will ever be able to stop at a given point in space and time to say, *I Am*; for only Jesus, Himself, could ever accomplish that. However, this should not preclude us from trying to lift-up every sector of the Earth and sky in His same high kindness, mutual civility, emotional convalescence, racial reconciliation, and wholesome purity. We may never be able to look toward God in our mind's eye and tell Him that we are already perfect; but this does not imply that portions of our thoughts, words, deeds, and actions cannot be *perfected* in Him. When we nourish the hungry back to the fullness of good health, His same perfection is springing from us, too. Indeed, should we be so fortunate as to mediate a dispute toward averting an armed confrontation which might otherwise have resulted in a massive loss-of-life, we have also deployed the Victory of the Resurrection of Jesus inside our hearts, as well. We can be heroes and saints for God here on Earth, at the same time we try our best to avoid pitfalling into temptation and sin again. Even those who have spent years and decades savoring the ruttish habits of the flesh can be converted into the realms of spiritual excellence, if only they will tender their entire constitution to responding to the overtures from God. I, for one, am a believer that from out of the worst mortal despots can come the greatest contemporary conquerors for the Kingdom of God on the Earth. Jesus Christ is perfect; and we must be perfected; while every ounce and fiber of our being, each second which passes-by; and our fullest potential must be directed toward redefining ourselves in His Holy Name so as to minimize our error to its smallest degree. We may never quite eliminate it altogether in our brief span of years; but our momentum must live inside this intuition if we expect Him to recognize us when it comes our time to die. If we tell Him in Truth that we have taken the initial steps toward understanding the meaning of His Divine Love, even in our stone-cold blindness, He will consume the balance of our weaknesses by the power of the Cross and deliver us midflight the rest of the way into the fullness of His Light. In this prospect, our honest intentions are often as effective as our trophy-case of achievements in setting other people free. Were it not for such hope and our penchant for change; for destiny, meaning, prayer, fortitude, pain, and daring; we would have all been damned long before we ever set-out to try to make this world a better place for all facets of life to endure. When our minds grow weary and our aching craniums feel the fashioned pressure of daily existence bearing upon our temples, we must realize that this is God at His best, reckoning our hairlines with the measures of His Love to determine the sizes of our Crowns. Hereafter, if there is no hope in our hearts, we shall not find it anywhere!

The matter of how we engage Heaven is what our mortality is all about. Some of us only stand and wait; and this is equally as benign a station before Him because our Ruler and Maker will place us wherever He chooses us to be, once we are fully absorbed by His Grace. Those who may rise to greatness in human affairs, the influential magnates of global economies, and the humble souls who hover elsewhere in the secrecy of their rooms all comprise the legitimate ascension of humanity toward reaching the date-certain when Christ shall reveal what the true meaning of our mutual fate has really been all about. The essence of this point is that we are all important to Him; each and every one who stands either upright with distinction or somehow postured by an improper poise; there is not a soul alive who is anonymous to the God who gives us life. And, we are responsible to know this well; never forgetting that the lives we lead in private will eventually be laid bare before His Throne so as to be seen by those who surround us now. So, why the wait to become the human family that we will ultimately be forced to embrace in Paradise; or else risk being cast like dice against a gritty brick wall to the sound of screeching cat-calls in a darkened alley called Hell? Our popular nature, facility of judgement, deposit of wisdom, and the very sanctity that keeps us whole must be a culmination of the taming of our waywardness through our espousing of the homiletic Beatitudes; because Jesus Christ is in no mood to barter, bargain, or negotiate with those who wish to conduct their lives according to any other code, while somehow expecting to assimilate the reception of the benisons of God in the end. By all means, this leads to the inevitable conclusion that we have somehow placed the back of Christ against the crass millstone of Creation; and His patience is growing very thin. It is as though His Nativity was the sound of the Door of Eternity gently becoming ajar; His Passion and Crucifixion are His promise that we are freed from terminal exile and the curse of certain death; His Resurrection is our venue for deliverance back to God; His Ascension has given us the thrust to reach the Firmament; the Pentecost is our Wisdom to convert all other men; and the Hosts of Paradise are hovering in midair above us now with their angelic wings flapping, waiting patiently for the utterance of our response. Indeed, it does not take bull-horns, airwaves, and cell phones to give Him our answer; just a simple whimper from the bottom of our hearts that we have finally noticed Him; beyond all the disorder, distractions, and clamoring that we have generated to keep us occupied. The eery-dead silence that haunts the majority of peoples around the globe today must sound like the winds passing across the headstones in a dark cemetery somewhere when God lends His ear to determine whether we have ever decided to accept His Love again. Where is their faith? What has happened to our courage? If fear is to be man's legacy, let history record that it was galvanized in our age.

William L. Roth, Jr. has penned *White Collar Witch Hunt* to ensure America and the greater world that the Original Catholic and Apostolic

Church is, indeed, in the authentic hands of Christ. William is not some quixotic hero who has come forward to somehow miraculously repair the image of the Church in a day when it seems so appropriate for the secular world to be collectively putting Her piety down. There are millions of Catholics around the globe who have placed the very Salvation of their souls in the power of the Sacraments. Evangelical Protestants, naysayers, and doomsday cultists who have been trying to diminish the supernatural power of the Roman Catholic Church for hundreds of years have never succeeded in placing so much as a chink in the armor of Her Crest. There are no cracks, clefts, or fissures in the Truth as it still stands aright; for Jesus Christ is always at the head of His Table of Sacrifice; His Immaculate Mother is gently caressing the Holy Paraclete, the Saints are still marching to the cadence of the Sacred Liturgies, and the Angels in vast numbers continue to be our protective advocates in the realm of the spiritual unseen. William has stated that this is not a time for panic; but we must certainly not stand idly by and allow the Catholic Church in America to be scorned and castigated by the secular government and the paranoiac media because of the failings of a few. Let the record be clear; *there can be no acceptance of the scandalous nature of the relationship between our priests and the unwary innocents who are placed within their care.* William has written this book not in an effort to condone any wrongdoing by any Church officials; whether they be the clergy, their advisors, counselors, or even the laity, itself. It might be easy to cast-off the ongoing assault against the Roman Catholic Church as being some radical ultra-conservative, right-wing movement of religious zealots who are filled to the brim with self-righteousness and an agenda of destroying anyone who might be different from them; while the Catholic priesthood just happens to be their next victim. However, the Church Hierarchy has already admitted that there are faults within its ranks. There is no denial or rigidity inside the Magisterium; but the idea that the actions of a few-dozen sinners should somehow cause the devolvement of the grace of an entire group of over 47,000 holy priests in America must seem an awfully lot like a modern witch hunt to God.

It must never be said that anyone involved in the Church is not sorry for the pain and suffering which has been imposed upon the victims of those who have molested them. The Roman Catholic Church will never assume a state of objection about the facts; its leaders will not attempt to coerce those who have been afflicted to remain silent; the individuals who are considered to be pederasts will not be allowed to hold positions of pastoral or ecclesiastical authority over their flocks anymore; and the proper preventative processes will be placed into action to preclude any such persons from actualizing such tendencies again. However, those who humbly answer the call of God to enter religious vocations are not even slightly the clandestine *whited sepulchers* that some people have painted them to be; and neither do they seek professions in which they will be surrounded by wine and roses so their self-esteem might be inflated before the rest of the world. Our Catholic seminaries and convents are inhabited by generous and loving Christian men and women who have been led there by Jesus Christ, Himself. If anyone in America today demands that our prayer rooms should be filled only by vestal virgins and our sacristies with beatified mortal men, perhaps they should look toward eradicating their own transgressions, instead. There is no systemic corruption or any endemic flaws in the vocation of the priesthood as an institution for leading humanity back to God; rather an unrelated case-by-case series of incidents wherein certain individuals have fallen to the wicked influences of the flesh. However, since most common citizens have no means by which to control the erratic lust for power and wealth that the media stand to generate from this unfortunate set of circumstances, the rest of society will be wrongfully led to believe that the austere men who have entered the priesthood are helplessly enslaved by an uncontrollable homoeroticism or some other psychosexual dysfunction. Thank goodness, those who understand the realities of God and His Faith-Church on Earth know better. While these holy men pour-out their lives for the sake of His Kingdom with the mark of the Crucifixion on their souls, the rest of us will grow old and gray someday, sitting on a spindly wooden bench in Central Park, tossing bread crumbs to the warbling pigeons, wondering why we did not do more to help Him in the past. We know that our children learn only what we bother to teach them. America is silently telling its impressionable youth that the practice of homosexuality is somehow alright by us, hailing such deviancy as being normal conduct in our advanced Western democracy. Those we lead into such aberrant behavior rarely go on to marry in adulthood, so they search for another meaning in life. Thereafter, when God calls some of them into religious vocations, they continue to be haunted by the cruel malignancy of their secular childhood; so we subjugate, defrock, prosecute, and imprison them as though they are the infarction of all humankind who must be ultimately excised from within our species and tossed into the fires of our own hatred to finally be destroyed.

     Therefore, I agree with William L. Roth, Jr. that we as concerned American citizens should not allow the institution of the priesthood to be assailed as though everyone who has entered it is unfit to serve in any other capacity in society. Lest we forget, this Nation exists to worship God; and the converse will never be true. We have become a breeding ground for rogue existentialism, countless pragmatic agnostics, secular materialists, social extremists, and a boisterous collection of nitwits who act like we have nothing better to do than implore our Almighty Father in Heaven to leave us alone and let us have our own way. When William Roth addresses the spiritual obedience and Divine submission in which we are supposed to be honoring Our Lord, he is quite correct in maintaining that our opinions were never solicited by Jesus Christ 2000 years ago when He surrendered His Life on the Cross after saying, "...It is finished." He never reached into the 21st century to inquire of us what portion of His Commandments we might wish to decline. When William discusses the Sacraments of the Roman Catholic Church, he is speaking about the very elements of our immortal sanctification. All that is loving, charitable, exculpating, pious, sacrificial, and virescent about the Tree of Life by which we are sustained is found in the Mother Church; led amidst Feast and temperament by our holy priests, their Reverend Fathers, and the Supreme Pontiff in Rome. We owe them our strong allegiance; our prayers, support, admiration, obedience, and consolation as they serve during these last of times to usher Jesus Christ into His Creation once again. It was, indeed, an unfortunate tragedy on New York's Long Island in March 2002 when Father Lawrence Penzes was shot in the back and killed while offering Holy Mass before the Altar of Sacrifice; not only because of his death and the mourning of those who loved him, but for the parable it left behind about what many in America are attempting to do to the priesthood at large. We must hope that *White Collar Witch Hunt* loudly sounds the clarion Truth that there are yet many thousands of sacred people living among us; not the least of which are the multitudes of Roman Catholic priests who are trying their best to condition our pitiable souls for the Final Judgment of God.

Timothy Parsons-Heather
June 2002

Section One
Robed in Majesty

Chapter I
Spiritual Obedience and Divine Submission

"Archbishop is not a corporate executive. He's not a politician. It's a role of pastor. It's a role of teacher. It's a role of a father. When there are problems in the family, you don't walk away. You work them out together with God's help."

Bernard Cardinal Law
Archdiocese of Boston, Mass.
February 2002

So begins the struggle to heal and help; to restore, support, regain, redress, and forgive. Should we not hereafter recall that our every facet of reconciliation, the recollection of our human dignity, and all new revelation are founded within The Divine Mercy of Jesus Christ? Indeed, the Roman Catholic Church is not even slightly inclined to be evasive or reluctant to accept responsibility for bringing this tragedy of unfortunate proportions to an amicable closure through every ameliorative means possible, ridding itself of the possibility that it might ever occur again, and willing to sustain the proportionate reprimand for failing to preempt this unforseen attack of evil upon the very chosen priests who are charged with administering the Holy Sacraments of the sanctification of humankind. After all the smoke from the explosion of these circumstances has cleared and the fog of what is yet unknown has been lifted, humanity will see that there has never been an ounce of corrupt motivation or arrogance in the Hierarchy of the Church with regard to the unequivocal task of seeking spiritual piety over matters of the flesh in our search for full unity in Christ. The world will also see the true immensity of the foundations of our faith, and whether these withering times will reveal any remnants of hidden goodness that we are yet reluctant to extol. Let us all pray that there will be many layers of benevolence still blooming inside our "beings," and that these will be the new blossoms of hope that every man and woman desires to see once the entire deposit of mortal history has been exposed. When our benign and sympathetic expressions seem too meek to embrace the glorious Easter Resurrection of the Savior of our souls, it is quite fitting for mortals from every walk of life to discover their consolation in the Immaculate Mother of God, who offers the prophetic comfort we find so lacking in one another. Mary can transform the youthful innocence with which we attached our crepe-paper streamers to the palm-grips of the tricycles that we peddled so innocuously in our small-town Easter parades decades ago into the powerful mightiness of a foamy cascading falls, the deafening percussions of victory resounding in the skies just overhead, and the steamy plumes trailing behind the salutatory warplanes flying aloft which rattle the rolling meadows below them in accompaniment to our *Pater Noster* prayers in glorifying the Most Sacred Heart of Her Sacrificed Son.

It would be grand to behold if our personal diaries were to become filled with more than just a chronology of eulogies for our greatest hopes that too often seem to simply pass beyond the dusk; but that they might also be a living tribute to the things we have done well, a commemoration of the true contemporary greatness of a responsive human species who finally discovered our final cohesion in unity and peace through the pristine Doctrines of our Messianic God. Not everyone alive was so blessed to have been reared inside the protection of a loving nuclear family or a community that was given to the simpler things of life, let-alone a parish sanctuary that espoused interpersonal Love over the mundane expressions of our newspaper headlines and cultures. We who are Christians must make our canticles and liturgies come alive again by embracing the traditions of Roman Catholicism; learning again the immeasurably mystical grace of the Holy Sacraments, genuflecting before the presence of God instead of offering only a casual curtsey or a momentary pause in our gait; and elevating the humble men who are serving their priestly vocations so that our souls can be purified and Redeemed. We are all subject to the temptations of sin, including the clergy; and we are also required to bow in deference to the expunging power of the Sacrament of Confession, no matter whether our memories, grudges, or prejudices may try to convince us otherwise. Let's set the record straight: Roman Catholic priests might fall as individual transgressors at times; but they are definitely *not* a collusive group of conspirators against the dignity of humankind the way the detractors of the Church, including the predatory media, are trying to describe them these days. It seems awfully strange that the victims of such extraordinary circumstances are holding their allegiance to Jesus Christ hostage until the secular world intercedes on their behalf in judicial courtrooms around the country for their own financial gain; and yet, they believe that this same Holy Church expunges their sins the moment they exit the confessional while they are never required to relinquish a penny to any mortal man or their God above who has dispensed with their error at the intonation of their confessors' voices. Satan must have said to himself in the earlier centuries about his desire to destroy the Roman Catholic Church, *...if only I can lay waste to her priests, I will own the venue to cease her desire for the Salvation of man.* Thereafter, he knew to tempt the followers of righteous faith with the spoils of the flesh; for this is how evil has deposed empires, evangelists, and emperors; it is why the secular elect have returned to their alma maters with their tails between their legs, it is the reason so many exceptionally decent people have surrendered the fight to regain their personal purity, and it is how the most well-intentioned executives and international leaders are exposed as puny weaklings and subjected to the occasional trial of public rebuke and congressional impeachment.

There is no doubt that Satan's lust and lies are the barnacles and parasites that are still trying to cling to the hem of the Holy Church as she walks upright amidst a world of such treachery and deceit. Surely the forces of evil wish to avenge the loss they suffered when the Son of God resurrected the souls of humankind from under the carnage of our own sinfulness and left our transgressions behind as fodder for the damned. Let there be no doubt; the priesthood cannot be destroyed by the failings of a few. No sensational twisting of the facts by the printed press or by any television medium will ever so much as leave a trace of a stain upon the raiment of piety in which Jesus Christ has clad His Catholic Church. The Original Catholic and Apostolic Church is both supernatural and invincible before the onslaught of a world of sinners because her King is situated high above the celestial Firmament in a splendorous excellence we cannot yet see. While our Baptism renders us clean of the reproach of our birth, the future of our Eternal Salvation is stationed completely in a Land of the Living that we shall never touch while in our mortal flesh. And, this is what we should be seeking as a unified family of man; not a blind retribution or the sending of battalions against the origins of our errors, or the tragedies they produce; but an infinite search for paranormal justice in the personage of God, Himself. How do we accomplish it? By the remaking of our own consciousness toward the purpose of becoming worthy in His sight to receive the Most Blessed Sacrament, the Holy Eucharist, from the Altars of His Roman Catholic Church. So, let us gather as a humble community of faithful citizens who would so overwhelm our priests with our desire to receive the Bread of Life which is consecrated at their hands that they should yield no idle moments in their daily hours for Satan to ever attack them again. We spend too much time investigating the doubtful, creating false impressions, debating resolutions against the Truth, condoning inconceivable wrongdoings, defending personal corruption, embracing illusions, casting dispersions, and speaking in profane and uncivilized veins of tawdriness; all to the purpose of feigning a posture that is of no more noble service than either our frail capacity to change the universe might portend or our fractured insolence would have us avow. The fact remains, however, that the spiritually-inquisitive nature of every new generation will always lead us to discovering the Truth about God inside the exculpatory ancestry of the Roman Catholic Church of Christianity.

We are more than a mere pittance of the complacent commonfolk that we often perceive ourselves to be; for in us rests a greatness that only our desire to know God can extract. There is not a soul alive who cannot generate a capacity to become identified with, in, and through Jesus Christ for the power we need to conquer the world. But, the normal course of human events renders us shy of assuming that God fully knows and sees what we are doing here on Earth; and the patterns of our reclusiveness places us wholly at odds with the conditions and circumstances that make His inclusion the better part of our waking hours. Should we ever see our way clear to acknowledging His primary requirement for our spiritual obedience and divine submission in heeding His Sacred Word, we would be swiftly on the road to understanding what human life really means. This is why we must begin to do everything within our reach to staunch the hemorrhaging of what little dignity and personal good will we have left in America and around the globe today. By all means, standing in alignment with the charity and servitude of other men for the cause of our Christian alliance would be quite an appropriate place to embark. We are called to engage this propriety, no matter what our chosen faith; because it is clear that nothing else in the physically tangible universe has ever allowed us to retrieve the invisible spirits of those who have preceded us in death. We are required to submit to the admonishments of those who own a closer understanding of Christ; and this is the earliest precognition that we can be internationally connected both intrinsically and explicitly to the translucent Kingdom of our Divine Creator. It is also first and foremost the reason why God's priests in the world must embrace both bachelorhood and celibacy; to the goal that only their perfected union in Him can be the reason for their lives. God will never defer to allowing His servants to be distracted by any other vocation than to serve Him with every ounce of their being, i.e., priests other than those whose spouses have died before they were called into the seminary cannot simultaneously engage the vocation of their ordination and that of becoming the master in a home of any biological children. Aside from those who decide to remain single for reasons known only to them, mortal men must choose either fatherhood or the donning of clerical vestments to ever be successful at one; but not both as a concurrent profession. It does not take a clairvoyant to know that the Saints in Heaven are not married, even if they had previously exchanged such nuptials before they surrendered their souls in death. Indeed, as we ask our priests to show us what it means to become a saint, are we not mandating them to become the very likeness of Jesus Christ, Himself; who was a bachelor through the very instant He Ascended into Heaven on the 40th day beyond His Paschal Resurrection? When we ask our priests to "...be Jesus" for us, are we not requiring them to be equally as chaste and sacrificial, as well? There can be no doubt that the Holy Spirit is their constant companion through the tortures of daily life as they pour-out their souls before all humankind in the likeness of Our Lord. The recitation of their homilies, the reading of the Gospels, the offering of the Eucharistic Prayers at the Holy Sacrifice of the Mass, administering the Sacrament of Marriage, presiding over the Rite of Christian Burial, and all their other religious offices are the script that Jesus has written for them to vocalize atop the world stage as the unfolding of His Creation continues its final course.

Let us remember the prescriptions that God has given us through His Judeo-Christian passages, *"...there is an appointed time for everything, a time for every affair under the heavens. A time to be born, and a time to die; a time to plant, and a time to uproot the plant. A time to kill, and a time to heal; a time to tear down, and a time to build. A time to weep, and a time to laugh; a time to mourn, and a time to dance. A time to scatter stones, and a time to gather them; a time to embrace, and a time to be far from embraces. A time to seek, and a time to lose; a time to keep, and a time to cast away. A time to rend, and a time to sew; a time to be silent, and a time to speak. A time to Love, and a time to hate; a time of war, and a time of peace."* (Ecclesiastes 3:1-8). When we are searching for patience, forgiveness, pardon, and peace; we must never forget that there is a season to everything; and it is through this broadcast perspective that we must view our service as mortals inside the parameters of our faith. The Church is permanent and timeless, and we are the modern custodians who must protect it for all future generations to come. What this means for us is that we own the responsibility for maintaining its purity without scandalizing its trust. We are called to guide our peers without casting them out. Jesus Christ must surely be telling us through the power of the Holy Spirit now that this is our time to be born again in mutual Love; a time to heal, a time to build, and our moment to laugh and dance in the Dawn of His Easter Resurrection. This must assuredly be our time to embrace one another forever-to-keep and to stitch our consciences to the silken fabric of a newly Redeemed humanity; for this is our opportunity to speak loudly in the way of the Apostles, and is our shining moment on the hilltop of the galaxies to heal each other and seek Christ's final peace. Should not the God of our fathers castigate us with every fiber of His Divine Being if we should fail to recognize these times about which He has so evocatively spoken for thousands of years before? Can we not sense the many directions we are being dispatched and the depths of mutual forgiveness to which we are subtly being called? Are we too partisan-blind and lacking in spiritual foresight to know that we are being attacked from all directions in this 21st century by the scourge of evil works, prodding us to hate one another until the ages ultimately come to a close? This is why we must perceive the Church, its priests, and even the laity-in-service in a much broader scale than the weaknesses of a few; and in so doing, we will be capable of acknowledging the timelessness of its grace beyond the immediacy of our individual faults. The Church is comprised of sinners who are struggling to become the likeness of the Saints; with angelic hearts, pure intentions, and high moral aspirations. We must begin to engender a renewed filial affection for one another as a fruit of our overall Love; evolving ever closer to being kindred both in spirit and mutual friendship through our Redemption in Christ—forever redefining what the rest of humanity means to us in reflection of our creation by the same God who sustains all life.

For all her contemporary accidents, the Catholic Church has never once surrendered her maternal, majestic, eminent, and infallible role of intercessor between Heaven and Earth; and no human error, misgiving, miscalculation, or brief loss of focus will ever be able to destroy her as the source of all infinite consolation before the dignified presence of God. Such a perfect ascension for the future of humanity will continue to be dispensed in Creation through the Wisdom of the Holy Spirit, established by Jesus Christ to be prevalent beyond the last vestige of man; sustained by our faith, empowered by His Love, and emboldened by the Passion and devotion of His Eternal Sacrifice upon the Cross. Our Lord is in all and everything that is perfect within us; and we are only now realizing that our intellectual judgment must bring us to suddenly pause, retract our arrogant objections, and allow Him to finally succeed. This is the only way that the societies of the Earth will ever be united; by embracing the Son of God who has been anointed the *Christ* for every man, woman, and child; not beholden to any form of fashion, whim, or deceit; gratified by our own servitude, glorified through every form of human obedience, and who is yet anticipatory of the full arrival of our wilful consent to accept His salutary Blood. If Saint Andrew's cross is the shape of an *x*, and Saint Anthony's takes the form of a *T*, then surely the Cross of our Divine Absolution upon which Jesus Christ was Crucified marks the exact Pneumatologic Crux where God commands us to greet Him in contrition while taking-on our brothers' weaknesses as being not completely unfettered from those of our own accord. Is this not what Bernard Cardinal Law was saying when he asserted that we must work-out our difficulties together, with the Holy Spirit of God as the adjudicator of our course? If we do this as one humanity again, there will be nothing remotely immoral about achieving our self-actualization, so long as it leads to a better understanding about the Commandments of God, and not to an inordinate advancement of the self over the progress of any other peoples, either socially or of the material realm. Our search for perfection must begin in our willingness to accede to the requirements of other individuals to prosper not only for the goods they need to survive, but also by placing them beneath the same garment of forgiveness under which we protect the reputations of those we love the most. In essence, therefore, we are required to absolve anyone who has offended us as a matter of factual grace; and notwithstanding our personal discriminations against the identities or vocations of those by whom we may have been so sorely defiled. Jesus requires us to pardon everyone who has transgressed against us, lest we find ourselves undeserving of His vindicating advocacy before His Father when our time arrives to die.

It is incumbent upon us to teach our brothers and sisters the art of living Love by projecting it ourselves. There can be no trace of vengeance in our motivations that would serve to further indict our enemies. If there is to be a heightened cohesion between us in the evolvement of our mutual trust, we are required to become nothing-less than the beatific Incarnation of the Christ-Child who once lay in the manger of Bethlehem. Therein rests the intrinsic nature of our reason for having faith; to Love humanity even beyond our own comprehension, superceding our ability to perceive the fullness of God's Kingdom from here, and knowing deep inside that His supreme omnipresence will ratify our ingrained acceptance of His Holy Will and guide our future through the domain of all that is yet to be revealed. Therefore, we have nothing to lose by granting our unconditional forgiveness to anyone who has burdened us; for it is better to believe that this is what Jesus wishes from us now than to carry our grudges beyond our graves and suddenly discover that our stubborn reticence is His tangible evidence that we have rejected the very foundation upon which our own Salvation has ultimately been laid. It is because of this Truth that I have written this book; so as to teach my fellow men that we are called to be perfected; but we are not yet perfect. Those who serve us behind the Altar of Sacrifice were helpless sinners long before they became the great giants, legends, and heroes that we recognize them to be today. If we are betrayed by any one of them, it is because there is still a great deal of work to be done in contrasting the world as we wish it to be and the one for which we remain reluctant to lift our morning prayers. Do other people fall to certain sins because God was awaiting *our* petitions to keep their temptations in check? If we would have asked Him to elevate our priests above the snares of the urging of the flesh long before now, would He have surely done so? No one alive is completely blameless for the failures of the entirety of all humankind, for we are summoned to hail the Mother of Jesus Christ as the intercessor for the mortal Earth and those in Purgatory, too; the same Blessed Virgin whom most among us would rather disregard as having any role in our spiritual refinement and Redemption at all. Is this the price the world is now paying for casting Her assistance aside? It is not beyond the purview of possibility that the end of time will reveal that countless men and women have failed in their fight against evil because it was the *rest* of us who declined to remember them to God when we were selfishly asking Him to render His assistance to only ourselves, instead.

We tend to forget that our own mortality will eventually kill us, so we must never be deceived into believing that the world passes-by too slowly sometimes. On the other hand, we too-often exploit the brevity of our years as an excuse for grasping everything within reach to make our lives more comfortable. No authentic submission to Heaven above us will allow this to be our goal because Jesus has refocused our divine potential to become quite the opposite; urging the growth of our higher spirituality, selflessness, suffering, deference, loyalty, and prayerfulness. The Pope in Rome knows this to be true, as well; as he is as concerned as anyone else who owns a worthy conscience that the egregious events of the past few years might cast a pall of darkness and doubt over the future of all good priests. While speaking from the Vatican and Saint Peter's Basilica on March 21, 2002, Pope John Paul II described the scandalizing of certain parishioners by their pastors and parochial vicars as a horribly catastrophic event. *"As priests, we are personally and profoundly afflicted by the sins of some of our brothers who have betrayed the grace of ordination. They have succumbed to the most grievous forms of the mystery of evil. Grave scandal is caused, with the result that a dark shadow of suspicion is cast over all the other fine priests who perform their ministry with honesty and integrity, and often with heroic self-sacrifice. The Church shows her concern for the victims and strives to respond in truth and justice to each of these painful situations.* "(Catholic News Service). There is no mistaking that the Holy Father is unquestionably on the side of those who have been afflicted by the sins of others, but he is equally as concerned that the world not be cordoned into the poise of assuming that every priest would ever fall to committing these same types of transgressions against those who have been entrusted to their pastoral, custodial, and ministerial stewardship and Catechetical guidance. There is no question that after all the casualties have been enumerated and the fulness of their grieving has passed beyond the darkness of the ages, the integrity of our faith will be sustained and the Church will finally prevail against her evil adversaries. This hope is the charismatic nature of our religious profession; and it keeps our spirits alive through the substance of our prayers.

There seems to be an almost infernal repugnance to the world we greet everyday, but our submission before God does not require us to take it lying down. The elitist forces of apathy and secularism which try their best to defeat our faith are grave enemies to the Love of Jesus Christ; and the genuineness of our desires to prohibit them from impugning our spirituality is a strong barometric measure of whether we are more apt to concede the battle of keeping them at bay, or if we will eventually acquire a certain loftiness that will hold our souls so close to Holy Christendom that nothing of malevolence could ever bring us down. Our existence is defined by how we manage to carry ourselves through the mine-fields of despair which usually accompany the fight for greater world peace and the fullness of communal Love. We are nearly guaranteed to be heartbroken if someone despises us for extolling the Scriptural Virtues, especially if it is a long-time personal friend or a group to which we belong by whom we have been recently disclaimed. Such is the sacrifice we make for honoring the Savior of the World before any mortal man. The practice of Christianity is a lonely business these days because it seems that there is nothing else on Earth that is so opposed. When we dress ourselves to go to Mass on Sunday morning, others are packing their coolers and filling the fuel tanks in their cars for the long trip to the football stadium so as to be sure to get good seats along the sidelines. Many more are holding ice-packs on their heads in the process of convalescing after a raucous Saturday night in the bars and discotheques. Believe me, I know first-hand from my younger years how this kind of agony hurts. Maybe most every Christian sitting on a pew in church used to be a part of these things, but we have matured into the realization that such are only passing fads and the wasting of too many important hours of our lives to continue that way. If our spiritual faith is to be taken more seriously, we cannot allow ourselves to be unmindful about the suffering of those who cannot even see past their own brows from pathological blindness, people sitting in wheelchairs from crippling diseases, and our impressionable youth who are starving for mentors to keep them off the mean-streets in the middle of the night. Our modern teenagers like to keep the wheels rolling on their flashy automobiles, just so they can hear their tread-pattern singing against the pavement as they travel down the boulevard. But, their transition into adulthood is inevitably a few years away, just like we are now; and they will recognize the futility in seeking a life that is separated from God. It is only after we come to know what it really means to be the little children of Jesus Christ that our souls finally discover what is truly worth seeking in the end. There is no doubt that we can remain childlike in our demeanor when certain circumstances warrant it—indeed, the Holy Gospel makes this very clear. And, then, there are times when the full maturity of our faith must take-hold as we become courageous warriors against the labyrinth of evil forces who are trying to besiege the propriety and decency that Our Lord wishes His Kingdom to espouse. The wiser course is knowing how to live a hybrid of the two by remaining simple in our conduct and valorous against the atrocities which try to diminish our faith.

There is a consortium of innocence and premeditation that every Christian should adopt, never allowing our temperament to become either too callous or eccentric as our understanding of the Divine nature of God reaches its higher peaks. Indeed, how the fiends around us will try to take advantage of someone who has given their entire consciousness to Him is when we are called to be equally as vigilant as we are trusting that His Holy Spirit is always our protective guard! The product of the intersection between our spirituality and the everyday world is that the definition of "normal" changes once we have accepted the Cross. Christians place the order of the day into a more conducive light, comparing the distractions we see before us that are put there by the enemies of the Church alongside the Truth as it is fully divulged by Jesus Christ. Therein, we know to never compromise the aspirations of human Salvation or confuse the definitions of right and wrong in order to gain the acceptance and admiration of a certain societal clique. We can never pacify the eternal yearning of our souls for the origin of human life with anything other than the sweetness of God once we have finally savored the freedom of His Love. Thereafter, anyone who speaks to us in enigmas about their version of the meaning of their existence seems almost as fickle as the ranting of a Canadian goose. What is the central point of all this? That those who have entered religious vocations have already overcome such things as these mosaic diatribes which are designed only to distract us from seeing the perfect connection between humanity and the Throne of our Creator in Heaven. They now reside among the upper-crest of spiritual benefactors to whom the rest of us should listen like paupers about to be given the secret combination to a deceased millionaire's safe or our state's winning lottery numbers a day in advance. They are in close proximity to the affections of God; and we are the fortunate lot who are unworthily blessed to be in their midst. Such priests and other clerics are His postulators who recommend their predecessors in death through their majestic oratorical unctions and prophetic readings before the Church tribunals to seek the blessing, veneration, and canonization of new Saints and intercessors; the same Hosts of Paradise whose personal prayers before the Face of God might be the only reason we are considered worthy in His sight to be pardoned after all. Herein, no one would call for the repressing of their standing ovations by reason of any objectionable moral, political, or militaristic grounds because the *censer* in their hands emits the Holy Mist of our contrition before the Slain Messiah who is the consummate Judge of everything that is seen and unseen. It is through the advocacy of our Roman Catholic priests that we discover that the motley visage of humanity-redeemed glows just as brightly in the here-and-now as in the blinding Light of Paradise, which helps us shed the worries of the world in favor of a more spiritually regal attire; for the Mystical Body of Christ who lives partly beyond their tombs and uniquely united with us who have yet to die is the summation of God's reclaimed children in a singular bassinet. Our giddy innocence is a byproduct of the shared suffering that our priests assume as a portion of their unity in Christ so we can take our castanets in hand, skip the melodious fandango, and go merrily on our way. When they offer us God's absolution within the confines of the Penitential Rite of Reconciliation, this is precisely what transpires.

Our Salvation is our Heavenly Father's personal reward for the intentional begetting of His Son, sending Him to the Earth to die, and trusting that we would believe that He has been raised from His own grave for the purpose of renewing our allegiance to Him, bequeathing our souls to His Sacraments, and leaving our corrupt flesh behind. It was certainly a disparaging fate to subject our Savior to, but it must have somehow seemed mysteriously appropriate in the Eternal Plan of God. Hereafter, we can rest in the solitude of His peace; but certainly never on our laurels, because there is still much work to do to convince the rest of the world that our faith is aright. There are far too many hungry mouths to feed, infant children left unattended, the elderly who lay unkempt, wars to terminate, souls to purify, injustices to eradicate, fields of dreams to sow, and entire races of people to deliver intact before the enamored Cross of human sanctification.   Our spiritual obedience is the seamless manifestation of our actions toward accomplishing all of this in the name of Holy Love. And, where can we learn how? By envisioning the examples that are living before us now in the priests of the Roman Catholic Church; they who serve for decades in forsaken places around the globe as missionaries; the ones who are bludgeoned beyond reprieve and left to die by evil thugs and atheists in the doorways of their sacristies; the noble men who are forced to dodge the hailing crossfire in the streets of old Jerusalem; they who crawl through mangled forests beneath the snakes dangling in the trees to reach someone whose soul is starving for the Most Blessed Sacrament; the humble servants of Jesus Christ who awaken at 3:00 a.m. and recite the Holy Rosary; and the tens-of-thousands more who work the clock around to Christen little children, visit homebound shut-ins, attend to the dying beside their hospice beds, hold the lame and lonely in the mountains of Croatia, lift the impoverished to dignity in the streets of Bangladesh, rescue forgotten paupers in the gutters of New Delhi, and convince the despondent to spare their own lives in the dark alleys of Amsterdam. Such servants are the living presence of the compassion of Jesus Christ in mortal humankind; and they do not deserve the indignity by which they are being stricken from haughty journalists who are witch-hunting for scapegoats in the name of "daily news." They are a blessed consistory of helpers who are stationed between the Gates of Heaven and the gullet of flaming Hell; a place we call the Earth, the bedrock of our mortal home; who trek across the countries where we live, to the cities where our outcasts go to bleed and die from raw violence in the streets, and into the dungeons where arrogant aristocrats have incarcerated the condemned from within their midst and segregated the "...least of these" who have been banished from their sight. When a Catholic Bishop lays his hands on a candidate for ordination and pronounces him a "priest," the whole world becomes a more sanctified hall of grace because the Resurrected Son of God owns another soul to fight for righteousness. However, there are rarely any front-page columns reserved in the *Morning Pantograph* for the thousands of holy men who have held true to their sacred vows of chastity and obedience because writers and publicists cannot capture their millions of dollars in capital profit-sharing by applauding holiness.

It is apparent that there is a modern-day contempt and outright loathing toward Catholic priests in America today that is spasmodically eructed from the belly of the secular world because these humble clergy are a curse upon those who live in direct contravention to the Beatitudes of Christ. Their entire vocation is a high commentary for the rest of the world because some people see them as snobbish elitists from some ulterior cult. The media and the common man on the street would wholly benefit from a reminder that God is on the side of these disciplined apostolates; and He could not proffer a tinker's dam about what political party wins a certain election, where the World Series will be held next year, or whether it seems too hot along the Floridian coastline to host the Masters Golf tournament. The transformation of humankind into the likeness of Jesus Christ is His only concern for now; and the priests whose souls He has distended across the breadth of the Earth for the administration of the Seven Sacraments of the Roman Catholic Church are the most powerful among us to whom we owe our faithful gratitude. We know that some of them can fall at times; but the prospect that they will rise and stand again is conditioned upon our proclamation that their service is worth the cost of rescuing the remnants of their dignity which the world is trying to destroy, hoisting them upon the broadness of our shoulders, and carrying them across the chasm of their momentary weaknesses until they are back on their feet again. If we ever disassociate ourselves from every family member, acquaintance, personal confidant, or stranger down the block who has offended us; we would be walking through life as severed isolationists inside a prison of our own indignance. We never really do this to anyone; and our priests should be among the first with whom we reconcile. If our divine submission and spiritual obedience is to be worth its salt, there is no doubt that we must perceive our priests as being among those whose souls we take under our strictest confidence. We should refrain from rendering remarks that might scandalize their appearance before the masses for *all* the reasons I have outlaid in the pages of this chapter. The pain and agony of the memories of those who have been offended by the few who have fallen to temptations of the flesh must be expunged from the record because no one alive knows the true degree of their contrition or their status before the Sacred Heart of Christ. There is not enough ink in the world or pages upon which to apply it to write the many blessings that the leaders of the Church have wrought from the hands of Almighty God for the healing of humanity-on-the-mend. If it would be possible to place every flower that has ever grown in the history of Creation at the feet of the Immaculate Mother of God, it is also Her prerogative to request the gift of Her priest-sons to be collected under the protection of Her Sacred Mantle, too. We cannot convince the Virgin Mary that we love Her, and that we accept Her as our beatific Matriarch, if we decline to pray for them every time we bow our heads or see the vast castellated clouds on a bright, sunshiny afternoon and think of the beauty of the Deity in Paradise who deigned to suspend them there. Once our full legacies have been inscribed, beyond the stripes of human encroachment, past the imbedded permanence of battle scars and massacres; Eternity will forever remember the servitude of the Church through the affiance of the noble souls who have donned the Roman collar for the purification of sinful man. We are the wounded Adam for whom their lives have been sustained; and Jesus can hear them now, just as He sees every other child; calling from beyond their own fragility to give them near-superpowers to fight for the sake of His Kingdom in the likeness of no other age. Therefore, when we see a man strolling down the sidewalk or through a revolving door at the entrance of a skyscraper somewhere who is wearing a black cassock and a white collar around his neck, we can be unerringly assured that he is robed in the majesties of God, and that our hearts are the target for his works. Let us help them all succeed, despite our lackluster gratuitousness to be of little assistance in conjoining them in prayer; and at least to the point that no one should hinder their progress for the conversion of their flocks. Not a soul alive shall please their God by castigating those whom He has chosen to effect the spiritual ministering of His people in exile; even in the depression of their more disingenuous hours; for they are each and all His disciples for the elect. Would we be so worthy before the Holy Cross as they who are His priests, there is no doubt that we might call for the early effectuation of Psalm 63, in the seeking of the Christ to whom we owe our lives before another dawn.

Chapter II
Our Declining Vocations and Exodus En Masse

"The priest continues the work of Redemption on Earth...If we really understood the priest on Earth, we would die not of fright, but of Love... The priesthood is the Love of the Heart of Jesus."

St. John Vianney, *Cure of Ars*
Catechism of the Catholic Church
Part Two, Article 6-VII, 1589

Surely most everyone alive has either seen or heard of the scripted scenario that depicts an old man slowly swaying to and fro in his rocking chair on a squeaky hardwood floor and a feisty tomcat positioned right behind him with its tail wagging under one of the rockers in a rhythm that allows its furry appendage to be relocated to safety just before the weight of the chair arcs across the floor again. Would we not assume this to be a parable to describe how close the entire world is to being crushed into unadulterated oblivion by the unexpected revelation that God has finally had enough of our indignant obstinance against the priceless Divinity of His Church? There is a great deal more of our mortal existence evolving just beyond our senses than we sometimes care to accept; for our souls are created in the Kingdom of God's Dominion long before He places them inside the fruitful wombs of our mothers upon the auspicious occasion of our prenatal incarnation. This is a secret process to which we are not privy because humanity is blind as to how our invisible spirits are formed. We do not know whether we are constructed by a phasic process resembling the assembling of girders or wooden frames like a transparent building, or if there is a sudden "pop" somewhere beyond the higher universe and we suddenly come into being. Suffice it to say that God owns His plans for manifesting the objects of His making; and we, quite inexplicably, are part and parcel of the result. We can be sure that there is an irreproachable Light of Love that shines upon us through this entire course because there is nothing slightly dark about the creative genius of the Triune Creator of everything righteous that exists. The degree to which we understand and accept Him, however, is reserved for our own personal accord. As I have indicated in the previous chapter, many among us have become the giants of Christian leadership and apostolic zeal, while others are so far from God that they would be required to research His Holy Name in the dictionary to discover the meaning of the term. Indeed, after doing so, some among us are disenchanted with what they read, close the book, and snicker over the misfortune that they even wasted their time. It is quite a sorrowful set of circumstances to know that some people refute the fact that the Holy Spirit of the same God who gave them the breath of life would somehow condescend from the heights of Paradise to infiltrate the very sinners He once condemned. This is why He makes our acceptance of His interior Reign a voluntary concession within each one of us. Heaven would leap in jubilation that we might be so receptive in conquering our own proud corruption without Our Lord and Savior having to beg to come in!

There is nothing of any substance on the face of the globe that is worth pursuing if its origin is illicit in the judgment of God; but many people have a penchant for traveling down such fruitless avenues anyway, just to experience what appears to be brief satisfaction in the short-term as opposed to waiting in hope for certain triumph at last. Such individuals are entirely confused about what it means to be a true visionary of human greatness because they are only poking their noses through the cracks of their humid cellars of self-ingratiation, rather than enjoying the broadest view of the purpose of life from the penthouse verandas of their better-intentioned conscience. It is an unfortunate facet in America today that the imposition of such tunnel-vision upon the psyche of our youth is leading them away from holiness like rodents following a pied-piper. They seem to base their goals and objectives more upon the temporal, tangible, and expedient; rather than the interior spirituality that would make them more productive in establishing a curriculum of isagogic studies based upon the principles of Christianity. With such a lacking in their personal mission, it is no wonder that so many of our preparatory schoolchildren are so wistful and melancholy about the prospect of discovering the reason for their birth. Modern-day parents are being forced to compete for the respect and attention of their offspring against the influences of American manufacturers that make our children's toys, video games, faddish apparel, and foodstuffs. While we are attempting to direct them toward a more comprehensive relationship with Jesus Christ, such profiteers are doing their worst to persuade them to decline our efforts in favor of an ambiguous realism that has nothing whatsoever to do with the Christian Church. And now, with the onset of a higher number of single-parent families being the trend, the disciplinary standards which marked so much of the generations before us have all-but disappeared because such adults are absent from the household, working in the labor-force to pay the bills. Does this not leave their sons and daughters on their own to learn about the responsibilities of personal obedience and civil decency? The fact that mother and child may be separated only by a simple cellular telephone conversation does little to amend the fact that there is hardly any interfacial communication between them anymore. Indeed, the prospect that adolescent children might attend Church on Sunday with their mothers and fathers in the United States today has become nearly extinct because of the other activities with which they have filled their schedules. Is it any wonder, therefore, why so few young people living among us are being acclimated to accepting God as their first priority of the day? There is a certain cause-versus-effect relationship that exists in practically everything we do these days which may, at first blush, seem quite benign. Our fathers dispatch their sons to the soccer field or to baseball practice with the hope that they might become so successful in these sports that they will discover a career there and make them both ungodly rich. All the while, the roll-call at our Marian prayer cenacles and formalized Catholic Youth Organizations is becoming smaller by the day in a nation where the population is growing by quantum leaps for every census. The result is that there are so few young men attending the Holy Sacrifice of the Mass anymore that the Church has been forced to resort to allowing their female counterparts to serve as Altar attendants for their priests; the effect of which is that fewer adolescent boys are becoming exposed to the sanctifying power of the Holy Spirit of Jesus Christ, who would otherwise be leading them to entering the seminary and onward into priestly vocations of their own. To make matters even worse, the little girls who are serving in their stead are now claiming that *they* should be allowed to be ordained in the absence of a sufficient number of males; a position which is wholly rejected by the Church Hierarchy.

All of this has contributed to the incidence of declining vocations in the western hemisphere, where we claim to be about 90% Christian, with an expanding number of over sixty-million Roman Catholics in the United States alone. Additionally, there can be no doubt that many of our other choices, both thoughtful and wanton, are diminishing the effectiveness of the Church and our station before God in the same broad stroke. Has anyone ever stopped to ponder that if only a fraction of a percent of the unborn males who have been aborted in their mothers' wombs since January 22, 1973 had entered the priesthood, we might conceivably have as many as 15,000 vibrant new ordinations by now, and every parish would have a pastor and multiple parochial vicars to tend to their ecclesiastical needs? This number is based upon the probability that at least half of the aborted fetuses in America are of the male gender. What if we all arrive before the Face of God at the end of time and hear Him tell us that He had intended to make the other half, composed of His innocent little girls, holy nuns in the lineage and likeness of Blessed Mother Teresa of Calcutta? One would think that we in America have taken the idea of reserving our right to choose what we wish for ourselves and our nation so seriously that we have unwittingly and arbitrarily decided to be self-redeemed through some other venue than the Holy Cross; even though it is quite obvious that there is none to be had. However, once we have become conspicuously aware that the Sorrowful Crucifixion of Jesus Christ is our only means to Eternal Salvation, we are thereafter mandated to accept Him openly, volitionally, uninhibitedly, and absent of any pseudo-exculpating caveats we might desire to append. The cardinal virtues of justice, prudence, temperance, and fortitude always take a giant leap forward in time once somebody else finally understands this Truth. Are we required to look any farther than the annals of history to see that it is quite ominous when we are in the presence of a fellow sinner who has rejected the Holy Paraclete as their interior counsel? As soon as the words of nullification pass their lips that they have refused to be bound to the Divine Laws of God, it is as though we can see their souls plummet through Creation like an asteroid on its way to slamming into the surface of Jupiter. All we need to do is witness the mourning and grief that is borne by the survivors of the many tragic events which have pelted our own planet to realize the horror of having a brush with death and being unsure of our immortal station before the Lord. Imagine being aboard the Uruguayan Air Force F27 turboprop airplane flight that was carrying the Old Christian Brothers rugby team of Montevideo in South America to Chile for a series of games in October 1972 which crashed in the 18,000-foot Andes mountain range. There were forty-five people aboard, five of them women, when it impacted the summit of one of the peaks, causing the loss of twenty-nine of them, some who died almost instantly, and others who eventually succumbed to physical exhaustion, starvation, and exposure in the cold of the higher elevations. A broad-ranging search for the plane was conducted for an extended period of time, but was terminated after it was determined that there must have been no survivors, and the actual location of the crash-site could not be firmly established.

An unsuspecting farmer working by himself near the Village of Los Maitines heard a small rock drop near his feet alongside a foothill stream some ten weeks later, not knowing that this event would have a greater impact upon the fate of the remaining passengers aboard that Uruguayan airliner than any number of random asteroids that might have shaken the foundation of Jupiter-in-orbit. Attached to it was a scribbled message from two young men who were too weak to shout across the water. When the farmer looked to discover the source of the note in his hands, he saw them standing on the bank at the other side of the stream wearing rugby cleats, with their frostbitten palms waving in the air. Indeed, they were Roberto Canessa Urta, age 20, and Fernando Parrado Dolgay, 23, who had breached the Andes with little food for their journey and insufficient time to sleep, announcing that they had survived the airplane crash, along with fourteen others who were still huddled in fear and anticipation at the site of the wreckage, where they had been weeping, suffering, and praying to God for deliverance during the previous 70 days. Without the determination that Canessa and Nando brought to bear upon their sanctioned lives through their faith in Jesus Christ, they would have never made it down the mountains, and they and their friends would have perished as a result. As the great radio-journalist Paul Harvey might say, "...and now, the rest of the story." The survivors of the airplane crash made an accounting of how they stayed alive for ten weeks in one of the most hostile environments ever known to mankind. The most important of all the details is that the entire group of them recited the Sacred Mysteries of the Holy Rosary of the Blessed Virgin Mary at night while they were nestled together inside what was left of the plane's mangled fuselage. They melted fresh snow in the daytime-sun for water to drink, and were forced to cannibalize the frozen remains of the deceased for solid nourishment. An avalanche struck them unawares in the predawn hours one evening, which took another toll of them to their deaths. It was only after one of the young men told Canessa and Nando that God had revealed to him in a vision that they would be saved that a spark of new hope began to flicker. He told them before they began the long journey across the untold number of precipices of the upper-Andes that they would make it through, and that they should not stop walking until they arrived at the "green valley," which they eventually found to be the lower mountain shallows where the farmer was working. There is no doubt inside the heart of anyone involved in this story that the intercession of the Mother of God is the reason the remaining survivors were rescued from the incident. The two boys who made it to the valley were Her messengers of reclamation, healing, and revelation. And, this is precisely what God has made of His holy priests among us; because we are slowly dying in the wreck of this broken world, and they are the chosen ones who have been sent by Him to announce the arrival of His good favor. Our Divine Creator tossed a stone into the physical universe which became the boulder that Jesus Christ moved so He could walk alive and well from inside the Sepulcher on Easter Morning where His loved-ones had laid His Body the Good Friday before. Indeed, He is the Cornerstone and the Word among us with whom God has enfolded the celestial globe for His people to proclaim; to reveal to us that there are vast societies aplenty in need of our immediate assistance, lest they die as forgotten heroes; as ignored and neglected as the pitiable contingent of agonizing souls who crawled from under the carnage of their faithful companions in that fallen aircraft high above the Uruguayan plains.

For what other reason would God allow those poor individuals to be forced to consume the corpses of the mortally sacrificed victims around them to stay alive than to lead us all to the Sacred Flesh of His Crucified Son from the Altar of the Roman Catholic Church? From what alternative source could either Fernando Dolgay or Roberto Urta have garnered the strength to make it to tell the rest of the world about what was proffered to them through the strength of the Love in their hearts? They were God's couriers who conquered one of the most cruel and indignant terrains in the world to pronounce that humanity has been called to render aid to everyone who is trapped in poverty and in dire need of help. Was Jesus telling the entire deposit of Creation that now is finally the time to cast the first stone against our own mediocrity to finally wake us up; not because we wish to condemn anyone else, or that we are not sinners anymore; but because we require the attention of all mortal men to become aware of the plight of our agonizing brethren in our midst? If we turn the calendar back another sixty-years to 1912 when the RMS Titanic departed Southampton, England and struck the iceberg which eventually led to its foundering beneath the darkened fathoms of the icy North Atlantic, do we dare reckon that God may have somehow ordained that there would be an insufficient number of lifeboats for the manifest of passengers by half, and that the stately Carpathia would be steaming along four-hours away instead of the forty-five minutes she needed to get to the "unsinkable" vessel from Liverpool on time to rescue the 2,200 souls on board? It is quite obvious that Our Lord was looking for heroes then; and He is assuredly searching for us to be the deliverance of millions now. He allows us to fail sometimes so we can envision the blind shortsightedness of our plans, looking down upon us as we strain in horror to see our brothers and sisters dying while we listen to their wails of agony and hollow gasps as they struggle to take their last mortal breaths. Such catastrophic events make us become giants in the throes of necessity; and those among us who are our Catholic priests are not unlike the courageous men who stood aside and allowed the helpless among them to take their seats in the Titanic's lifeboats, just as Nando and Canessa risked their lives descending the Andes mountain range for days and nights in the blistering cold to save their friends from death.

If only we could instill this same sense of urgency in our young men of America today that this is what it really means to be a legend in their time, fit for induction into a communion of contemplative Saints, perhaps our sprawling land would be better primed for a renewed interest in the Catholic priesthood. Moreover, one is not required to live on alms alone to serve effectively in a vocation today because the Church does not mandate every reverend-father to take a vow of poverty or remain confined inside a monasterial calefactory for the rest of their days like many of their secluded predecessors chose to do. Local diocesan priests enjoy quite a range of social activities in their respective parishes, from the inner-urban cathedrals to the rural churches between villages and farms. Serving the needs of a spiritually-hungry parish can be quite a rewarding and gratifying experience, and not even slightly close to the running of the ecclesiastical gauntlet that many casual observers have chosen to believe. The problem that arises most often is that many priests are forced to delegate much of their spiritual duties to certain lay-people inside their parishes because they are too busy tending to other academic matters in regard to the parochial schools whose management has been placed under the auspices of the local diocesan clergy. There needs to be a protracted study performed to determine what, if any, of the actuarial roles respecting the development of the operating budgets, personnel selection and assignment, and the scheduling of the academic curriculum can be accomplished by the laity, above the consenting signature of the local parish pastor. The general consensus among a growing number of Catholics today is that the time has arrived to return the focus of our priests back to their inherent pastoral duties and away from the daily particulars of operating their respective parochial grammar and high school institutions. This is not to say that the priests in a parish should allow the laity to manage their schools absent of their proper adherence to the regulations of the Church, because some maverick lay-persons have an agenda of their own to "de-Catholicize" the function of the Roman Catholic mission. No one is suggesting, however, that priests should not continue to teach theology courses in the parishes where they serve; but some of the budgetary paperwork, processing of the bills, promoting effective public relations, and the physical maintenance of the facilities are items which can be suitably assigned to their employees and volunteers; all to the purpose of allowing parish priests to be given time to return to the prayerful lives to which God has been calling them since He first reserved their mortal existence at birth.

This certainly opens-wide the discussion about why so many priests have quit and resigned their vocations by the multitudes in the past twenty years or so, effecting an exodus en masse that would rival the evacuation of the student bodies from their classrooms during an emergency fire drill. Some statistics show that as many as fifteen percent of newly ordained priests leave their vocation in less-than seven years. Too many of them have bowed to the pressure that is heaped upon them by outside forces to exchange the inner-sanctity which they espoused when Jesus Christ first called them into the seminary for an expedient motif of some misguided ecumenical reform. Others just simply cannot understand why a certain faction inside the Church would implore them to relinquish the childlike abandonment through which they first answered the call from Our Lord to serve His Divinity from whence they were adolescent acolytes carrying the gifts to the main Altar during the Holy Sacrifice of the Mass. Some veteran priests fall victim to certain liberal focus groups composed of their younger counterparts who have been programmed by rogue leftist professors and theologians in the seminary to remove nearly everything that is physically and liturgically traditional about the Church from their sanctuaries, the Orders of their Offices, and from the Holy Mass, itself. Being too old to fight back, or too tired to face the opposition within the brief span of time before they retire, most of the elder priests and monsignors simply keep their sentiments to themselves, fearing that they might be left out in the cold when they need someone to care for them in their sunset years. Such human obstinance by the people who are intimidating them is not natural to those who profess to know God very well, and is not congenital to the reborn-elect who have been given new life in Him. Our trust for the entire lot of new priests can be reinstated when they stand firm behind the pulpit for the Catholic Truth which has been preached in homilies and in other public fora for the past 2000 years. How so? By the reinstatement of their strict adherence to the rules governing the conductance of extraordinary holy hours, the perpetual Exposition of the Most Blessed Sacrament, a regular and predetermined time that is reserved for the recitation of the Holy Rosary, the praying of the *Passionate Stations of the Way of the Cross* on Fridays during the entire liturgical year, and a stricter adherence to the regulations regarding fasting, self-denial, and the voluntary dispensation of the Spiritual and Corporal Works of Christian Mercy.

Additionally, other young men who are pondering entrance into the priesthood are harboring second thoughts nowadays because of the unfair stigma with which the profession is being effaced. The entire population of Catholics in America are bound under the laws of beatific propriety to ensure that any such errant assumptions about our priestly vocations are eradicated from our public psyche. But, this is not all that is happening to keep the number of new vocations at such low levels. In conjunction with the secular issues that I discussed earlier in this chapter, Satan is having a field day while in the process of capitalizing on the unfounded fears that he has generated in our broader societies about what kind of people enter our seminaries and the kind of priests they eventually become. Fortunately, we are so close to barging through his pretenses of smoke and mirrors that it would take a matter of only a few days to set the record straight. We are confused, however, by the occasional optical illusion that any goodness we might afford would not make a difference in sustaining the dignity of our clergy anymore because the evil around us has caused so many divisions and broken lines of communication in our modern-day world. All we have to do is look on our merchants' shelves and we can see this phenomenon clearly with our own eyes. Anyone who pays $999.95 for a certain product that he would *not* have purchased if it had cost an even one-thousand dollars has fallen victim to the obvious and discernable deception with which Satan is trying desperately to draw us all in. He believes that we are only a thousandth of an inch from selling-out our souls and investing in the corruption whereby he has laid waste to our personal morals, our national sense of decency; and our conscience, piety, and spiritual resistance, too. Such minuscule measures is all he needs to inhibit those who are leaning in the direction of entering religious vocations from taking that last step into the admissions office of their local diocesan Vocations Deans and signing with exclamation on the dotted line. To combat the effects of this diablerie upon the persuasions of our would-be new seminarians, perhaps it might be appropriate to revisit, expound upon, and echo the understood functions of our Catholic priests, beginning with the descendants of the early Apostles, as it is plainly accorded in the current Roman Catechism. Therein is clearly revealed the formal hierocracy, shared commission, co-consecration, and entrustment of the priestly vocation for the Bishops and their subordinate clergy.

1562   *"Christ, whom the Father hallowed and sent into the world has, through His apostles, made their successors, the bishops, sharers in His consecration and mission; and these, in their turn, duly entrusted in varying degrees, various members of the Church, with the office of their ministry. The function of the bishops' ministry was handed-over in a subordinate degree to priests so that they might be appointed in the order of the priesthood and be co-workers of the episcopal order for the proper fulfillment of the apostolic mission that has been entrusted to it by Christ."* (Part Two, Article 6, ff.)

1563   *"Because it is joined with the episcopal order, the office of priest shares in the authority by which Christ builds up, sanctifies, and rules His Body. Hence, the priesthood of priests, while presupposing the Sacraments of initiation, is nevertheless conferred by its own particular Sacrament. Through that Sacrament, priests, by the anointing of the Holy Spirit, are signed with a special character and so are configured to Christ, the Priest, in such a way that they are able to act in the person of Christ, the head."*

1564   *"Whilst not having the supreme degree of the pontifical office, and notwithstanding the fact that they depend on the bishops in the exercise of their own proper power, the priests are for all that is associated with them by reason of their sacerdotal dignity; and in virtue of the Sacrament of Holy Orders, after the image of Christ, the Supreme and Eternal Priest; and they are consecrated in order to preach the Gospel and shepherd the faithful, as well as to celebrate divine worship as true priests of the New Testament."*

1565   *"Through the Sacrament of Holy Orders, priests share in the universal dimensions of the mission that Christ entrusted to the Apostles. The spiritual gift they have received in ordination prepares them, not for a limited and restricted mission, but for the fullest; in fact the universal mission of Salvation to the conclusion of the Earth, prepared in spirit to preach the Gospel everywhere."*

1566   *"It is in the Eucharistic assembly of the faithful (synaxis) that they exercise in a supreme degree their sacred office. There, acting in the person of Christ and proclaiming His mystery, they unite the votive offerings of the faithful to the Sacrifice of Christ, their head; and in the Sacrifice of the Mass, they make present again and apply, until the coming of the Lord, the unique Sacrifice of the New Testament, that namely of Jesus Christ offering Himself once, for all, a spotless Victim to the Father. From this unique Sacrifice, their whole priestly ministry draws its strength."*

1567 *"The priests, prudent cooperators of the episcopal college and its support and instrument, called to the service of the People of God, constitute, together with their bishop, a unique sacerdotal college (presbyterium) dedicated; it is true to a variety of distinct duties. In each local assembly of the faithful, they represent, in a certain sense, the bishop, with whom they are associated in all trust and generosity; in part, they take upon themselves his duties and solicitude, and in their daily toils, discharge them. Priests can exercise their ministry only in dependence upon the bishop and in communion with him. The promise of obedience they make to the bishop at the moment of ordination, and the kiss of peace from him at the end of the ordination liturgy, mean that the bishop considers them his co-workers, his sons, his brethren, and his friends; and that they, in return, owe him both love and obedience."*

1568 *"All priests who are constituted in the order of priesthood by the Sacrament of Order are bound together by an intimate sacramental brotherhood; but, in a special way, they form one priestly body in the diocese to which they are attached under their own bishop. The unity of the presbyterium finds liturgical expression in the custom of the presbyters' imposing hands, after the bishop, during the Rite of Ordination."*

These promulgations allow for no uncertain interpretation that the vocation of the Roman Catholic priesthood is distinctly and successively united in the image, likeness, emulation, and service of Jesus Christ, the Savior of the World; and that they are the flowering maples of His forested ministry. Even yet, there are still innumerable citizens both in the secular and religious arenas who decline to give this "body of the priesthood" its deserving dignity or respect and, therefore, are consequently disparaging the holiness of Jesus Christ, Himself. No one is suggesting that priests are not sinners, but God is distinctly calling for the rest of us to elevate those whom He has chosen as His clergy and to be their advocates during their times of trouble so that we as the laity can fulfill our commitment to Him as their flock of communicants. There is no doubt that every parishioner is charged with the responsibility to never become a burden upon our priests, no matter to what degree of forgiveness they must be delivered; so that we who are occasionally as sinful to an equal degree might accept their ecclesiastical benison on

Christ's behalf. How can we expect the record of our transgressions to be purged from the backdrop of Creation if we cannot see our way clear to comply with what the Roman Catechism confirms with regard to the dignity to which Our Lord calls us to perceive His pious clergy before the vast compilation of humankind? Would the world not be more enlightened to realize that the very consignment of the salvific virtues of our spirits and souls rests upon the faith we place in Jesus Christ through the affection we maintain for the priests of His Church? Does it sound too difficult for us to concede that He has concealed Himself quite conspicuously in the poor souls who are suffering for the sake of His Kingdom, not the least of whom are those He has placed before us to be catalysts for our mortification and the perfecting of the sainthood that we have all yet to attain? It is quite obvious that the whole economy of the supernatural grace which belongs to the Church is offered through the sacred hands of His humble priests. Our contemporary western moralists such as Dr. William Bennett and others like him who often wish to quote Saint Augustine's *Order of the Loves* should be more inclined to recollect this in their rapport with our Divine Creator, rather than calling for the cessation of the tenure of our Roman Catholic Cardinals when the Faith-Church on Earth needs their wisdom and guidance now, more than ever. America should remember that our national conscience is empowered only through Christ's forgiveness of our sins inside the shedding of His Blood on the Cross; and nothing we might do to indict one another for not being worthy of such a vindicating miracle does anything to benefit the reason why Our Lord was so Crucified.

So, let the peaceful restoration of our Church begin anew; for it is only through the intercession of the Holy Spirit that the divination of our ecclesiastical works can be accomplished as one family of faith. If only we could garner more respect for the irreversible dignity of the power of God in those who wear the collar, we would understand why everything else that secular mortals do ultimately dies in time; and our obtuse actions should have never been allowed to start. In parabolic terms, no one among us can claim any control over the location of the Earth in the heavens; and thus we move our mechanical clocks ahead in the spring and back during autumn to take advantage of the reduced number of daylight hours. Americans otherwise attempt to resist any efforts to adjust our emotions, change our attitudes, curtail our obstinance, or amend our personal agendas to allow for the slightest particle of Divine Revelation to augment the substance of our Love. And, yet, some among us make it their sole purpose in life to persecute other people who have fallen to no greater darkness than they, themselves, have refused to resist. We live atop a world of arbors and admixtures, migraines and earthquakes, and sanctimony and sacrilege. Our sentiments are marked and collated by Kodachrome gulf streams and prismatic rainbows; untold crimes, passions, poetics, ironies, impudence, and almost inexplicable error. We allow our thoughts and hidden intuitions to play laboriously in the crispy heirlooms of the memories that haunt us everyday; grieving deeply over the silhouettes of bygone years, caricatures, and catafalques which bear the remains of the moments in life we loved the best. If we can be this romantic with the things we improvise that are only passing in the night and gone, then why can we not be as equally discreet in anticipating the inevitability of the bulwark of Truth before whom we shall be held accountable for every false revenge and distasteful vignette we ever entertained? Once we finally comprehend the relationship between the lowlands of our oppressions and the summits of our dreams, we will have finally cracked-open the meaning of life a little ways, just enough for us to realize that what is expected from us now surely exists somewhere beyond them both combined. So, if we become too callous when we are smitten by our friends and snubbed by our blood-relatives as we stand beside the Holy Cross like sentinels in the night; or if our bitterness makes our piety seem as flat as a desert horizon while we endure the wait for Jesus to come again, then it is "us" who cannot handle the overwhelming revelation of the Truth!

Never-mind the angst of not really knowing why holy people fall to temptation sometimes or why sacred shrines are pelted by gunfire in the middle of the night. If our lack of patience outgrows the determination by which we must see our victories through, then long live those who oppose us! The broader perspective and bigger picture of how God comes to us within the ornate order of His Kingdom and in the persons of our priests must surely be eluding us if we grow disenchanted with them through ordinary time; all of this while our human thought, writings, expressions, and personal experiences are only single planes on a higher landscape of supernatural design. Life often passes us by in slivers and slices as the sun arches overhead to force another night, but somewhere deep inside us all must live that perpetual glimpse of immortal reality which keeps our faith in God growing wide and ever-stronger by the day. We are unwitting to the details of the architecture of the universe, but our accidental discoveries are slowly growing our awareness of why the upthrow of Creation has been so finely planned; and we within it; for the moment, for history, for prophetic reasoning, and for that very last scintilla of Eternity which will finally reveal to all humankind what rests in the incalculable beyond. We are given the distinction to be seamlessly linked with all Divine potential by virtue of the Will of the Almighty Father, to enlist our participation in attaining that end to which every soul must ultimately arrive. Mere existence will not suffice for what we have set-out to do because we have been vested with a portion of the holy and the sacred inside the here-and-now. This is where our God chooses to emerge, and is why we must open the garden of our hearts like flowers to allow His power to sting us like a bee and, then, take from us the pollen of obedience to the distant fairfields beyond the skies. His ivory-crest Paraclete can see like the glistening of gold through the facade of our rickety alibis; and He knows when we are harboring dissenting sentiments about the sanctity of His Church and those to whom the responsibility for the conversion of our souls has been resolutely entrusted. If we wonder whether Jesus will take center-stage in fashioning the end of our world, we should extract the rudeness of our reservations right now and give Him the courtesy to declare that He has already been forthrightly presented to us through the Most Holy Eucharist, so delicately reposed in the tabernacles of the Roman Catholic Church. Indeed, the service and obedience of His priests is the only reason why.

If we hope against hope that our daydreams will come true, then the occasion of our arrival into the foyers of Truth when fully-divulged must become the refraction of the Love of God through the tempestuous whirlpools of our hearts. Therein, we are both conscious and aware that He has already immersed us below the high seas of His Grace; and what the world may bring thereafter; the legions of enemies knocking at our doors, flaming arrows in the night; whatever is of this malevolent age, none of it matters anymore because our faith, at least, has crossed the bar into the vast porticoes of immortal dominion, even though our souls are yet encapsulated by time, only one final heartbeat away from seeing it all come true. Our principle objective is to seek this Truth through Christianity and all that befits the service of humankind which goes along with living it. We should never be overly concerned where the lions sleep in the wild tonight or what may be the source of their insomnia, or how many steps it takes to walk to the marketplace, or whether the woman we met on the boardwalk this morning is wearing *Garnier*. Our Lord has left a contagious curiosity upon the brows of those who know Him best; for today is given to our prescient accession to His potency as to whether we can drink from such a fertile Cup without heaving from the gall. From now on, our mantras and serenades should be about refining this make-shift globe of artifice into a true and peaceful lovingness. Who, in the Name of God, has sufficient time to stand in idle picket-lines in front of Cathedrals against their fellow Christians when the entire face of humanity continues to be stained with the record of our arrogance, lack of self-control, penchant for material greediness, and outright reluctance in sustaining humble prayer? If the Holy Spirit would speak aloud to those who are so obsessed, He would probably beseech them to defend the Church in areas where they have wilfully let her down, and remind them that the God of our fathers has heard their type of pious platitudes before. This is our time in the ages to redouble and treble our efforts in upholding our Profession of Faith before those who have opposed it since they first fell collectively with Satan into the dark abyss of the netherworld in the stark reality of Good Friday. The descendants of evil are alive in our day; and they are throwing their fists into the air that they may be slowly rocking the foundations of the Church from under its pinnacles of peace and grace which are spiraling so stately among the clouds. However, they will not succeed in bringing her down because their efforts are in vain; their motivations are as dead as the Satan they embrace; and theirs is a future of eternal condemnation, far past the fires of Gehenna and into the broiling graves of Hell where all atheists and anti-Christians go. Secular penal institutions that would only castigate and incarcerate our priests are among the evil dogs who are surrounding them now, ignorant of the factual pardon that our fallen clergy have received before God through the Penitential Rite of Confession, and overstepping their bounds before His High Throne; for the Church is quite capable of conducting its affairs internally, relieving certain individuals from their obligatory duties, should that decision be an appropriate response.

If anyone wishes to know beforehand, Jesus Christ does not intend to leave His world this way before He comes again in Glory. There is much more to occur by way of spiritual purification—even chastisement, when it appears to be the only alternative course. We are not our brothers' judge; and neither do we own the right to publicly rebuke them if God has already preceded us in expunging any errancy which exists hereafter only in the bowels of our minds or our infatuation with premeditated vengeance. Only fools proclaim that there is nothing short of dying that will take away our sins, because the power of the Sacraments has already made us new. This, and only this, is how someone's soul can be transferred immediately into the Light of Paradise the very moment their spirit departs their flesh. There are no probationary appendicles affixed to the soul of a person who has received the gift of absolution during the Sacrament of Reconciliation which is dispensed upon a sinner by a priest. God would dare any other man to step from behind the crowded street-corners of the barbaric world today and affirm that he has such power! Should any one of them try, he would be speaking in the vainest form of blasphemy; for the granting of plenary absolution upon those who have yet to die has been bestowed upon the office of a Roman Catholic priest. We must pray that more candidates will choose to be ordained, and that they will serve their commission in flawless purity until the Son of Man should call them to their everlasting Salvation in the Glory of His sight.

Chapter III
The Embattled Secular World

"Our commitment to human rights must be absolute, our laws fair, our national beauty preserved; the powerful must not persecute the weak, and human dignity must be enhanced.... We have learned that 'more' is not necessarily 'better,' that even our great nation has its recognized limits, and that we can neither answer all questions, nor solve all problems....we must simply do our best."

Former President Jimmy Carter
Inaugural Address
January 20, 1977

A brief discussion about our American capitalist democracy would not be too irrelevant in citing the effects of the temporal world upon the function of the Church and the challenges which face the Christian clergy everyday. Divine Providence has it that the sublime explication of the parameters of human Salvation has been slowly engraved into our larger societies, wherein there are massive numbers among us who do not believe what the Holy Gospel proclaims. Nonetheless, we are required to continue living in the Light of righteousness despite our detractors; indeed, by virtue of our survival among them. Our efforts can never cease if we anticipate the expulsion of every form of error from within our midst for the allowance of everything that is pious about us to prosper without constraint. It seems as though we can never endure this process unscathed because there is so much opposition from the enemies of God, from those who harbor ill-will toward good and decent men, and from the ranks of the outright sorcery that is so prevalent in many quarters of the 21st century world. While the United States avows what seems to be a minimum desire for doing what is right, the real blockages to our surer spiritual conversion in Christian Truth expire at the courtesy of our capitalist democracy when it is at its best, i.e., when our freedom allows us to choose the courses of action that refine our societal ethics. However, this has also led to the manifestation of several demeaning stances and courses of conduct that are not really worthy of us. For example, no person of sound moral character would argue that the scourges of abortion and homosexuality are condonable in the higher subsistence of God. Our freedom to effect such choices may certainly make us unique among the other nations of the world, but it has also slowly eroded our stringent morality that has allowed the more attractive republics to shine in such esteem before the hosts of Holy Paradise and fostered their blessed standing for which every man should strive. If there is a departure from moral Truth today, it is a product of our refusal to resist the forces which make a mockery of post-modern spirituality. One might imagine that Jesus Christ would have keelhauled us by now for letting this fester; and the jury is still pondering the various reasons why He has precluded our many terrorist enemies from taking a much higher toll upon our native homeland; echoing the same destruction and factional dysfunctions that are ongoing in the Middle East and other hot spots around the globe.

The intersection of secularism and agnosticism has had quite a damaging effect on our international affairs lately because they are the common enemies of our Christian faith. But, they exist anyway, and we must learn to cope with their adverse impact while continuing our best not to destroy the domestic system of governing our peoples fairly because it is the only means we presently recognize for sustaining social order in a hemisphere with such vast diversity. As for America, itself, it is obvious that the best way to ensure interpersonal good will and provide for common respect between our citizens is for every one of us to become humble servants in the lineage of Jesus of Nazareth; a hope that seems a great distance in the future, at best. We rely on the power of the Blood of the Cross, our prayers, holy water, Bibles-in-hand, and the ringing of cathedral bells to remind us that our liberty to attend church as often as we wish is very much at our personal disposal. Even so, this seems to be not enough to purify our social conscience because too many Americans are electing to stay away from these faith-based institutions. Western secularism will remain only an end in itself if we do nothing to reverse this course because it can never inherently lead us back to the virtues by which we may become more holy and enlightened about the power of God over our private lives and the tangible environment that is in our immediate trust. This is the precise reason why our American democratic experience has heretofore failed to produce a more inquisitive population of spiritually receptive people. Many who have read my works already know that I have authored several other books, one of which is entitled *When Legends Rise Again: The Convergence of Capitalism and Christianity*. A portion of it compares the effects of secularism upon our compliance with the Sacred Beatitudes of Jesus' Sermon on the Mount. Therein, I have discussed our need to renounce the materiality that accompanies human life in America nowadays. I have noted that there are converse sides to this argument, too, because if we decline to engage in the causal profiteering that will grow and sustain our interstate commerce, we will unintentionally be defeating the progress of our national sense of purpose. We live inside the paradox of being forced to barter our goods and sell our wares on the open market so our friends and neighbors can feed, house, clothe, educate, and ensure the good health of their children; an economic system in which we, ourselves, have also become co-beneficiaries, while being called by Christ to seek a Kingdom of Love that is not of this world. Even as benevolent as this may seem, we are being forced to conduct the affairs of business by exchanging physical goods and manual services in order to survive; all while Jesus is telling us that the pursuit of such materialism is in direct contradiction to the ordinances of His Holy Gospel.

This is a portion of the conveyance by which I have described the meekness of our power to make substantive, identifiable, and meaningful changes to our modern culture that will take us closer to our union with our Divine Creator. It seems as though we are tending to our mortal existence by engaging in a broad financial base of fiscal profits and real property that is slowly reducing our spirituality to its lowest common denominator with every new asset we acquire. It is no surprise, therefore, that the Son of God has so little room to perambulate inside the "box" we have seemed to place Him in; from individuals who defy the call for social cohesion, to those who dismiss supernatural faith as a crutch for dimwits and paupers, to the mass-millions who would simply rather disengage discussing the question altogether. This is the agonizing face of social apathy that the Church and our priests are forced to combat. What our forefathers should have said at the outset is that in order to create a more perfect union, we must each and everyone strive to become a perfected people. This can only be done at the discretion of God through the invincible power of His *own* unique designs that are yet unperceivable through the length and breadth of our limited senses. No one is conceding, however, that the peaceful land of goodness that we espouse in our most optimistic imaginings cannot come true. For all the things that prohibit us from establishing the "perfection" that our founders dreamed about in their seminars and roundtable discussions, there are at least as many more reasons why we can still aspire to succeed. There has been a discernable reason for every dark avenue down which our nation has traveled; and the common thread to them all is that we have thickly plotted against the wiser courses of action and based the provisions of our journey upon what we can gain for ourselves over what we might otherwise reserve for dispensation to our impoverished friends or the succeeding generations who are silently imploring us to include them in our plans. Hence, we discover ourselves located inside another paradox again. Contemporary Christians must do something to ensure that all our defense mechanisms are in place so we do not fall prey to the maddening lust for greed and material gain into which our elitist capital solicitors are attempting to force us. The incessant barrage of mindless advertisements that are attempting to infiltrate our lives like a viral infection is quite a distraction for those of us who are trying to deny ourselves of their wares for the purpose of enhancing our relationship with God. Too many Americans are continuing to worship before the altar of opportunism and praying inside the temples of superfluous profiteering. The socioeconomic disparities in the United States today are not the result of some freak accident, but are a function of our sustained effort to capture the proceeds from our economic adventurism at the cost of denying a basic deposit of bare necessities to those who live in the societal margins. All of this is to the advancement of our secular age and the diminishment of the capacity of the Church to reach other sinners who are supposed to be heeding the Gospel with an equally commensurate emphasis.

It is quite difficult for our priests and other clergy who are charged with the task of taking this lesson of self-denial to the people to get their message across. They bear the Truth in their hands about the Theocratic Deity of sacrificial Love, but they are also victims of many among us who would just as soon shoot them for heralding the doctrines of Christian piety to the very people who need it most. This is why we should be thankful to God for His priests who embrace the holiness of their vocations, and commend to His Divine Mercy the remaining few who are not. Perhaps the Almighty Father might insist that a nation which has been built for the most part by the work ethic of a massive immigration of white Anglo-Saxon Protestants, also known as the WASP generation, should become less endowed with its own fanatical whims by relinquishing their brazen smugness to a humble college of priests. If we place this into a hopper for public consideration, Heaven knows what battle lines would be drawn. Judeo-Christian or not, the rest of us must admit that we have been just as guilty of valuing the glitter of our avenue storefronts over the solemnity of the Catholic Confessional, espousing private expediency over volunteer public service, and stockpiling our surplus cash inside our own savings boxes, rather than depositing it in the ecclesiastical collection plate. There is nothing even slightly subtle in our innuendoes of telling God that the extrication of our fallen souls from inside our darkened coffins is no more important to us than our reluctance to exhume the Silver Certificates and Federal Reserve Notes from the depths of our wallets to ease the plight of the poor. We listen to flowery speeches being delivered in public auditoriums, intellectuals talking about analytical theories in scholastic halls, and hear the trite political paraphrases of elected politicians; but none of them can equate with the occasional ring of Truth as it is spoken from a dying man in a hospital bed, a misguided child wearing handcuffs behind his back, or a feeble elderly lady trying to explain to a newly-hired teller at the local Savings and Loan where she has maintained an account for the past fifty years that she is who she *says* she is, while he denies her request to cash a counter check without a proper ID. Even by speaking and writing about these things, we run the risk of being criticized for thinking beyond the mainstream of the everyday world or embracing a deviation from the norm that is contrary to the ordinary way of conducting business as a personified group of patriotic comrades in our cultured hemisphere. We need to transfer our trust, faith, and allegiance more in the direction of our invisible God; and only by doing so will we be restored to civility, decency, and the innocuous essence of youth.

These are among the many problems that arise once we become too embedded in secularism; where we get our daily news from the skewed reports of the financiers who own the newspapers and television screens, losing track of those who are still among the living and those who are now deceased; where our nuptials are announced at cafeteria tables instead of in church bulletins; and where the charisma which has allowed what little decency we own to flourish amidst the echoes of our humble supplications to be overcome by the bustling noises of crackpots and revelers who have claimed a seat at the table in procuring a legitimized role in developing the fads and fashions of our general global mission and works of modern art. If only we would stop hypothesizing about the way life ought to be and take the steps to finally get us there, we would have less time for criticizing those who are trying to make the whole world a better place than their lazy counterparts who only speak snidely in their secluded arm-chair interviews. We would thereafter set-out to get our own hands dirty, ourselves; allowing our knees to become soiled in the process of laboring for our poorer friends once in awhile, and self-inflicting our own exhaustion in tending to the seedlings of those who have long-since fallen behind in cultivating a better future for the weak and destitute. It is alright if we complain to God that we are not 100% sold on laboring in such fields, as long as we arrive in time to make a small difference somehow, carrying our share of the load, and enduring our allotted portion of the physical aches and pains. Our actions always speak more loudly than our sentiments when it comes to matters such as these; and nowhere on Earth will we find better examples of those who serve so nobly in the trenches everyday than our Roman Catholic priests. If we stand along the sidelines and taunt them as they work, God will make us pay the price by handing us a burden so much larger than theirs that it will annihilate any obstinate syllables which would ever dare to crawl-off the back of our tongues. It defies all good sense and common logic for us to be bred to such insolence when most of us do little more than imagine what the world might be without the poor, let alone effect any changes that would see their numbers reduced by any appreciable degree. It would be a terrifying prospect to awaken some morning and discover that our priests are gone; every last one of them, and that the world was left to drift like a ship in the night without a crew, a battlefield colonel with no more troops alive, a razor without a blade, or a landscape painter who has suddenly gone blind. Would we backpedal to the ancestry of the Semitic languages and have no Manna of Life on which to feed? Might we decline thereafter to anticipate the resonance of God's bombardiers commissioning the report of His brassy trumpets to portend the imminent Return of the Proprietor of our souls? It is only through our priests that our lives are made more than orthodox and finely eligible for the grace by which we are saved, for they administer the Seven Sacraments of our purification for the bleeding secular world; in all its pain and agony, with its bland indifference and stark inequities, and the futile faithlessness of the many reprobates whose future is still in doubt; the globe is dressed for the rite of passage of all human ignobleness and the induction of the true reason for mortal life and the divinity of things to come.

Another fact that we know to be true beyond any hint of refutation is that God sees every man and woman as having the propensity to commit certain types of transgressions, either mortal or venial; depending upon whether we, ourselves, choose to embark upon suppressing the conditions which might lead us into them. Everyone who draws the breath of life, including private people, those who serve as popularly-appointed officials, civil libertarians, counselors, associates, and even multi-denominational clergy are not immune from being affected by the influences which can take us farther away from a state of grace. We are all susceptible because we have not yet fully embraced what it means to be the likeness of Divine Love, which can be none other than purely-flawless perfection. Let no one be deceived into assuming that Satan does not know what our weakness are because this is where he chooses to coerce us by striking successive blows to the bruises on our spiritually-fractured consciousness to the point that the power of our resistance seems nearly battered down. It has often been stated that a single incident is no more than an anomaly; two of a kind is a phenomenon; and anything beyond that becomes a trend. Jesus knows that we might fail once in awhile when our best guard seems to be low, but He expects us to rise once again and continue in Him with the intention of knowing better next time. Any recurring themes or circumstances that expose us as enemies of Love cannot be concealed for very long because the rancid nature of their sour fruits will ultimately despoil our relationships with our families and friends. Others believe that certain errata might be simple oversights, but our refusal to prevent their reproduction often causes our peers to be outrightly scandalized. Civilization would be better served if we could all agree that most of our common accidents are the result of unintended neglect and not a function of some premeditated conspiracy against the larger status of the world. Hardly anyone alive sits on the edge of his bed and formulates some type of proem or preamble to introduce his manifesto against humanity at large; although there have been certain exceptions to this kind of thought. The point I am making is that we seem to be constantly revolving in-and-out of unforeseen conditions in which we discover ourselves in need of rescuing for being nowhere in the proximity of Christian Truth; or if we are there, our souls need prodding not to stray too far from the dignity in which God has deigned to place us. Almost every conceivable action that we effect on the multiple planes of human existence somehow underscores our relative positioning in contrast to the defined dispensation of His Will as the Holy Spirit has chosen to expound. Much too often, we run short of the impulses that remove the blinders which obscure our better judgment because the visionary aspects of our spiritual awareness become distracted by the deceptions of time and the physics of the seeable universe.

When our understanding of immortal Truth has reached a point where it is completely irreducible, we will have then discovered that living in perfection means knowing the source of human Salvation as best as it can be divulged to any reasonable man. The predicate of this entire base of knowledge is Divine Love; not as love is defined with the expedience we might see in an antique nickelodeon or the type of puppy-infatuation that causes school children to pass secret notes to each other in World History class. The sacred Love that keeps us from falling into sin over and again is that supernatural obedience we offer to Jesus deep inside our hearts everyday; and this is the origin of the incomparable intercourse between Heaven and Earth which transcends our deaths before they ever occur. We shall never fully understand the fallacious faculties and spurious attributes of modern secularism until we realize that Christ holds the Dominion of His Love before humanity as the only medium for securing the fullness of Eternity in His presence. His Holiness, Pope John Paul II, has eloquently described this form of agape between man and God in his various homilies around the globe.

Therein, he solemnly resolved that, *"...the greatest proof of God's Love is that He loves us in our human condition, with our weaknesses and needs. Nothing else can explain the Mystery of the Cross. Christ's Love is more powerful than sin and death. Saint Paul explains that Christ came to forgive sins, and that His Love is greater than any sin whatever.... This is the Church's faith. This is the Good News of God's Love, which the Church has proclaimed throughout the ages.... God loves you with an everlasting Love. He loves you in Christ Jesus, His Son. God's Love shows itself in various ways. In particular, God loves us as our Father. The parable of the Prodigal Son expresses this truth very clearly. Do you remember the moment in the parable when the son comes to his senses and decides to go home? He sets off for his father's house. 'While he was still a long way off, his father saw him and was moved with pity. He ran to the boy, clasped him in his arms, and kissed him. (Luke 15:20) This is God's fatherly Love, a Love always ready to forgive (and)anxious to welcome us home. God's Love for us as our Father is a strong and faithful Love, a Love filled with compassion, a Love that allows us to hope for the grace of conversion when we have sinned. God loves all of you boundlessly, without distinction. He loves the oldest of you who feel the weight of your years. He loves the sick and those suffering from AIDS, and the problems linked to it. He loves the relatives and friends of the sick, (and) those who look after them. He loves us all with an unconditional, everlasting Love (i).... God alone is good, which means that in Him, and only in Him, all values have their earliest origin and ultimate fulfillment. He is (the) 'Alpha and Omega, the beginning and the end.' Only in Him can their authenticity and final confirmation be found. Without Him—without reference to God—the whole world of created values stay as though (they are) suspended in an absolute void. The world loses its transparency (and) its power of expression, too. Evil appears as goodness; (and) good is discredited....Why is only God good? Because He is Love. Christ gives this answer in the Gospel words and, above all, in the witness of His own Life and Death: 'for God so loved the world that He gave His Only Begotten Son (John 3:16).' God is good precisely because He is Love (ii)."* (i) Homily in San Francisco, California, delivered September 17, 1987; and (ii) Apostolic Letter to World Youth, International Youth Year, released on March 31, 1985.

Can we not deduce from these holy proclamations that the Supreme Pontiff of the Roman Catholic Church understands that the forces which are trying to destroy our relationship with Jesus Christ are no match for the desire of God to retrieve us as His own again? How would any pope feel as he looks across the Atlantic Ocean to see the marring disrepute of lust, promiscuity, and licentiousness which has become such an integral part of our western culture today? We breed it into the mentality of our youth from whence they are only adolescents; and we do very little to protect them from the influences that can only shear them of their baptismal innocence. Can the Pontiff not also see that we select a certain segment of them to become our spiritual vicars who are thereafter forced to battle the very psychological dysphoria that led them down the paths of perversion and turpitude before they ever came of age? While addressing the parenthetic assembly of American Cardinals about the tragedy of priestly sexual abuse, perhaps John Paul II might have reminded them that the lack of sound morality in the United States has forced itself quite disproportionately upon certain impressionable individuals who have subsequently chosen to enter religious vocations and manifested the trauma of their youth in later years in quite distasteful ways. The Pope reminded us that the grieving father welcomed his prodigal son back home because the latter's errancy was broken and he was ready to reenter the fold. Can we expect this same type of evolution to occur inside those of us who live in America, when we are the very mothers and fathers who are teaching our children to scoff at spiritual goodness and evade social propriety? If we continue to be so disengaged from the sanctions by which we are bound to Christ, how can we expect any other result than that our succeeding generations will resist the Divine Love which brought the Holy Father in Rome to speak with such truthful passion? The plural facets of our western secularism are not shining as brightly anymore because many of them have emerged as our churlish reminders that America is still very far from the grace of God. In His holy sight and the adjudication of His Messianic Son, are we not those whom the devil is trying to claim as his arbiters and principals? Indeed, is Satan not fostering the conditions that will allow him to calcify the emollience of our consciences and take us one at a time down to the cauldron of Hell to be dispensed like blocks of ice into the poisonous cocktails of his fiends and cohorts as they celebrate the addition of another condemned soul to the list of casualties in their putrid ranks? If we continue to defy what the Roman Catholic pontiffs have been telling us for generations now, this will be the fate of a massive number of Americans who seem to have nothing better to do than merchandise the malevolent influences that are driving our social culture into the ground.

Our determination and obsessive willingness to crawl into bed with uncontested evil has caused the proliferation of many secular violations, the most grotesque of which is the vast scourge of infanticide, also known as legalized abortion. The United States Supreme Court granted permission for our pregnant women to terminate the lives of their unborn children in

January 1973 as an acceptable means for controlling family expenses and easing the tax burden of the labor-force who would otherwise have had to pay increased welfare benefits to poorer mothers with illegitimate children. If anyone so much as implies that it was a function of any other derivation than the absolute greed of our people and the *intentional immorality* of the Justices of the Supreme Court, they are part of the same collusion of hatred against the dignity of God as those who are facilitating abortions. The fact is, the High Court had the matter thrown completely into its lap by reason of the exhaustion and denial of previous appellate rulings on behalf of an anonymous "Roe," and they were forced to grapple with having to weigh western decency against the fact that American women were willing to rip their unborn fetuses from their wombs with coat hangers and drown them in saline solutions in order to make their case for the right to choose. The latter is continuing to be utilized today as the ultimate lethal bath; the anti-baptism administered at the hands of the Antichrist. Not that this does anything to efface the spiritual stature of aborted innocents before God, but because such procedures inhibit the natural progression of created life to proceed unmolested into its fullest purpose. Such gruesome conduct cannot be equated with women risking their lives in hunger strikes or other such forms of self-mutilation to capture the attention of the courts because the execution of innocent life is being involved. When a sufficient number of licentious physicians, the Planned Parenthood Association, and other such malefactors were called to testify in 1973 that a first or second trimester fetus is not a viable human progeny, the Court had no alternative than to bow to the pressure of not appearing to know more about human reproduction and anatomy than those who had made it their life's career and livelihood. Our most intriguing and exquisite potential is to denounce such evil darkness and transfer the entire objective of our historical passage into the virtuous preparation of becoming like Christ. How we choose to deploy it, if at all, is entirely dependent upon the way we perceive the interrelationship between the invisible world of created existence and the obvious sights we encounter everyday. We cannot ask God what *He* would do in every circumstance because His end of our line of communication seems awfully silent sometimes. We know most often whether our prayers are answered because we can detect a definitive response or an essential alteration in the conditions which first took us to praying on our knees. We should never expect our petitions to be contingent upon how soon we see a reciprocation from Jesus because He holds the authority to amend both the merely subtle and most critical aspects of the material world as He deems fit to instate. It always benefits us to remember Him when we wish for personal prosperity because the possibility of acquiring an unforeseen inheritance or a fortune from random luck rarely proves to be productive for us. If we bet and win on the horses or hit the jackpot at our evening dinner-club, we could safely assume that it was a mere matter of chance, and not some sign from Heaven that we are in particular favor with God. The kind of blessings we are most likely to acquire are certain venues for addressing the needs of the suffering and infirm, even if we are charged with creating an entirely independent and self-sustaining apostolic mission to make it all come true. Our efforts toward accomplishing this goal are usually the perceivable signs of God's open response to someone else's prayers. This is how He makes our lives the deliverance of many segments of unknown societies that usually remain anonymous to us who live in remote locations around the globe.

We can force the brash phenomenalism that promotes the error of the secular world into becoming an unwitting partner in defeating the negative repercussions of its own pursuits if we hold it tightly against the backdrop of Christian religiosity. This is also how we can overcome the indifference of our opponents despite their efforts to appear to be in utter defiance of the Will of God. The potential I mentioned earlier can always be transformed into real tools for spiritual conversion if we counter-strike against our enemies by taking advantage of their lapses in anticipating our next act of Christian goodness or by playing on their naivete through which they may be underestimating our allegiance to Christ. If they are afraid to allow us to come within an inch of converting their friends to the Cross by drawing a secular line in the sand, His holy followers can always trump them by miraculously attacking them in their ignorance of the Truth from the other side of time. After all, this is what the Communion of Saints is all about. Christian Wisdom and spiritual mobility are not constrained by the deductive reasoning of worldly atheists because of the unbridled power in Deific Love. Anyone who proclaims that they love their neighbor with all their might but proudly refuses to believe in God is telling a boldface lie. We are required to love humanity with the same dedication that took Jesus Christ to the summit of Mount Calvary to die for our sins on the Cross, for His loyalty to everything His Father created; for our healing, protection, sanctification, and Salvation; and especially to provide us a permanent residence in the presence of our Divine Creator beyond our grave someday. This has not been, and never will be, achieved by any intellectual reaction or secular ideology. Indeed, only through the reduction of all apathetic improvisations from within our midst in favor of Christian assurance will the world be able to decipher the difference between the two. It is possible to see Creation with mortal eyes and still know what is expected from us beyond the invisible universe. The question is why we continue to decline the avenues that will bring this into much clearer focus. One might get the impression that humanity has been traveling down an unknown road in the dark while arriving at an unexpected intersection with a red octagonal sign imploring us to stop. But, once we have finished shredding the Truth into tiny bits and misconstruing what we see through our biased interpretations, the insignia before us looks more like an orange pentagon with a foreign inscription of *cesso* on its face; whereupon we disbelieve that God would speak a language other than what we might allow, so we stubbornly ignore the warning, proceed through the intersection anyway, and make the wreck of this world even worse. It is our opposition to His piety and Sacrifice that is allowing evil to continue to flourish today because purity and humility are always rejected in the secular world. If there is good will, healing, or the growth of those factors which contribute to the destruction of social unrest, it is because people who lead the charge on their behalf have given their entire existence for the sake of glorifying the Cross; fully aware that human beneficence can come from no other source. Such nobility is the higher meaning of life for our priests.

Chapter IV
The Canonical and Liturgical Hours

"They took away what should have been my eyes, but I remember Milton's Paradise. They took away what should have been my ears, and Beethoven came and wiped-away my tears. They took away what should have been my tongue, but I had talked with God when I was very young. He would not let them take away my soul; and possessing that, I still possess the whole."

Helen Adams Keller (1880-1968)
American Author and Lecturer
deaf and blind from infancy

With all the intensity of the interior of our being, Creation is called to encounter God from the inside-out; such that our very identity in Christ is made from the unity of Heaven and Earth through the heart of every man. What would He have us do to reap the riches of our spirits only from in Him? For this question, the answers run aloft, deep, and sorrowful; cultivating our awareness of the existence of the Universe by virtue of whatsoever we might accomplish to conjoin our lives with the Carpenter from Nazareth through the rightful suffering only we can bear. There has nary been a soul who would wish to know Redemption that did not desire to climb a mountain to map the green valleys below, or ford a stream to savor a salmon's flesh, tread with the African wildebeest, engage the hunt with falconers, soar alongside the cardinals' wings, and shun the world of the materiel to be consumed by the very essence of human life at the verge of leaving it all behind. The daily world we see at the compliment of our outward sight must never be perceived as the final product of our brief mortality, but often as the ulterior mare's-nest which would distract us from experiencing the Truth head-on. There is no doubt that the blossoming cherry trees and country lakes are quite beautiful to behold, but they are only the frontispiece to our anthology of life whose attractiveness might accidently skew our envisionment of what true Beauty really is. For this, we must turn only to Almighty God, for He is the Author of each and every one of these prudential landscapes that never fail to take our breath away. Would the venerable Helen Keller not also attest that the perfect line of excellence is discovered in the awesome wonders of the galaxies she came to know from within the depths of her soul, a Divine vision shared by her and God complete that is capable of raising us all from the crestfallen despondence we have inherited from the deformity of our wanton lack of piety? Who are we to say when the Earth is finally ended that the more important aspects for living might have eluded us from whence we first started nursing at our mothers' breasts in diapers until we breathe the holy scent of pardoning in the foyers of Holy Paradise? Will we waste the precious moments to which our years are given, and them to us, by sulking over being blinded by the darkness of our sins, instead of celebrating the glorious Light by which the victorious margins of our best intentions can be seen by the Princedom from on high?

This is not some abstract portion of theology from among the dying here on Earth because such meditative contemplations are the seed from which the purifying of our lands can grow. It is the inner-most constructive criticism of our mutual hours; that humanity should, and must, begin anew to coalesce through forgiving sins; to defy the discrimination, censuring, and condemnation of our fellow men which causes our struggle for peace to become such a fractured julienne of empty promises and broken dreams, rather than the unified bloc of hopefulness by which our God accords the answers to our prayers. These are the pondering sentiments that enter the thoughts of those who are called to serve the rest of us in righteousness; the young men who see God's sacred manifest of Saints beyond the skies while never allowing the scorn of the netherworld to seep past the lashes in their prayerfully-shuttered eyes; who cringe at the sound of clanging streetcars and stuttering auctioneers; and who beseech Our Lord almost desperately to make them worthy to be clad in the vestments of a priestly lot. They arrive there by the virtuous consent of the entirety of Heaven, of which our own petitions for them are nothing-less than the most vital part. Once the purpose of their lives has been defined from within the spiritual parameters in which they have reposed the laity of their souls, they are thereafter invisibly marked by God to be His warriors in the battle against human sinfulness. Indeed, this is the one and the same pure Truth which brought Miss Helen Keller to proclaim, even in her own infirmities, that she could perceive the Countenance of the Father much more clearly, concisely, and distinctly than did her peers through the soundness of their aptitudes. There is not a single iota of difference, thereof, in what she saw and the compliant Love from the Virgin Mary of the Theophanic Magnificat, the humble and scrupulous Maiden who would later become the Mother of our Incarnate God. With the incapacity to describe it in any other terms, this is the "touch" of the Holy Paraclete who gently plucks the souls of those who are blessed to become God's chosen ones in the material world like fodder in an eagle's grip, clutched firmly in its talons as He elevates them to the fairest form of servitude in the Hierarchy of His Church.

It is only through the flames of their humble submission and true humility that the holy tempests of Jesus Christ are inspired to blow in-kind and bellow His Divine Mercy of Love and Peace into the kilns of the cowering mortals who lay in sorrow upon the ground. Their laborious and perpetual surrender, consecrations, and sacrifices have led great numbers of their ordained counterparts to inscribe their impressions of how Our Lord has molded them unto His service, with many pious unknowns who remain entirely anonymous in their midst to see the Divine reflection of human Salvation emanating from their lives and pen it for all futurity, as well.

These holy men are given to an ongoing dialogue with Jesus Christ by the recitation of their morning Office and the offering of the Canonical and Liturgical Hours throughout the rest of their lives; every day, without omission or respite, lest they be negligent in their spiritual assignments and the provisions of their oath. I hereby proclaim that, upon the concession of every cleric who has ever donned the collar and miter of the Roman Catholic priesthood; if they will call upon the Most Blessed Virgin Mary for anything and everything they might require to succeed in the effectuation of their sacred mission; be it more strength to conquer the day, discipline to endure the night, humility to be self-subservient, or corporeal purity to remain among the chaste; then these things shall be given to them all told at the very intonation of their proclamation: *Hail Mary, full of Grace*! Our Lady of Love is our Holy Mother, and She knows how great is the distance between the agonizing steps of the journey of humankind through mortal exile to the edge of the River of Redemption in which we will be swept-away to our Eternal rest in Her Sacrificed Son. How foretelling it would be if the world should call upon this Queen of Heaven and Earth; therewithal the treachery in our pathways would be laid-low and bow before the Sacred Mysteries of God's never-forsaking superiority as it is revealed before the whole of humankind! Yes!..that we might hear the resonance of the Crown of O'Glory through the auspicious orations of the Immaculate Conception; for the groaning of the Earth cannot eclipse the adulating melodies of the Cherubim and Seraphim who all hover summa cum laude betwixt Her sabbatical entourage of faithfulness to humankind and Her pinnacled charity before the Angels above! The Mother of Jesus is the Matriarch of every papal, scriptural, spiritual, and supernatural Dominion to have ever been seated in command or authority over, beneath, and beyond the original founding of all the seen and hidden bastions, fortresses, landmarks, summits, chasms, meadows, prairies, and portals of God's manifested Creation. Her benign and beatific comeliness is the cynosure of every imaginable affection that is fit for an incorruptible human frame that the Almighty Father could possibly conceive in the span of His timeless life, or in a billion more eternities that might come-to-pass before the presence of His Throne. It would require nothing-less than another President John Fitzgerald Kennedy to be reincarnated on his most prodigious day and repeat before the world the essence of what he assured the sovereign States of America in Washington, D.C. on a blustery winter day in 1961 for us to understand what true commitment to our faith in Love really is. Reveling the strength of an entire human species to the higher nations of the New Jerusalem that is about to descend upon us from where he is now stationed in Paradise, he would gladly again extol, *"...let every nation know, whether it wishes us well or ill, that we shall pay any price, bear any burden, meet any hardship, support any friend, or oppose any foe to assure the survival and the success of liberty."* The pristine freedom he would exalt if we could only hear his voice from beyond the grave is that *we* are now the elect; and we shall soon be taken tassel and shoelace to the Feast Table of everlasting Salvation where all the Saints are now reclined. However, there are still some empty pedestals standing in their midst, awaiting our arrival, which look to the heart's eye prophetically like the 168 chairs at the site of the bombing of the Alfred P. Murrah Federal Building in Oklahoma City that was felled so catastrophically on the morning of April 19, 1995.

The rest of us might wonder where their survivors derived their strength to go on when it is apparent through the Christian Gospel that we are called to torture and eradicate every semblance of opposition to the Divine Will of God that may, at any moment in time, bring our hearts to question the authenticity of His Love. Such enduring is a gift from Heaven as we concurrently make our faith in Jesus Christ overwhelmingly worthy of all honor, dignity, and praise by requisitioning it from the very God in whom we choose to believe. It would be an outright apostasy for us to tell Him that we have the capacity to evolve Creation in our own right through a system of contingencies that are better than His own designs; or that the "roll and scramble" approach we often employ to avoid accepting the throes of mortal life, even in all of its painful aspects, should set us on the road toward searching for a false god who will not engage us to suffer such pain. Indeed, our every source of courage under affliction, resistance to temptation, and prevalent moral endurance is dispensed by the power of the Holy Spirit; the same graceful Light that allowed (the late) John F. Kennedy to steer a nation beyond the perils of a nuclear holocaust; the very identical fortitude that causes humble missioners of modern Christianity to be dispatched to remote and isolated places around the globe, and the singular Triune Deity who inspires receptive men and women to enter their religious vocations. All of this is the fruitful remnant of an interior life of undying Love whose origin can only be the power of God. How do we know this to be true? Because, as we learned from our early childhood, the Bible tells us so. When the world comes seeking the Scriptural authority by which we are speaking about the gift of the Holy Spirit at the center our hearts, we can openly direct them to a number of various passages so they can see for themselves what Truth is deposited there. *"Whoever loves Me will keep My Word, and My Father will love him; and we will come to him and make our dwelling with him"* (John 14:23; cf. Revelations 3:20)....*for behold, the Kingdom of God is within you"* (Luke 17:21). So that there will be no question, the St. Joseph's Bible confirms that the Greek preposition translated as "among" is equated with the signature of "within." The point is, the entire Holy Gospel is replete in emphasizing the spirit of the heart; that Our Lord comes knocking there to reveal the verities of His Kingdom to the lost. We are implored by Him to *"harden not your hearts,"* so as to remain open to the Holy Paraclete of immortal perpetuity, rather than conceding to the call and cravings of the physical flesh. The entire matter revolves around the virtuous presence of righteousness within our midst; one which cannot be procured through the material world. Anyone who attests that they are a child of God while remaining steeped in such possessionism is in violation of the Holy Gospel according to both Saints Matthew and Luke, *"...do not store up for yourselves treasures on Earth where moth and decay destroy, and thieves break-in and steal. But, store up treasures in Heaven, where neither moth nor decay destroys, nor thieves break-in and steal. For where your treasure is, there also will your heart be."* (Matthew 6:19-21; cf. Luke 12:33-34). *"No one can serve two masters. He will either hate one and love the other, or be devoted to one and despise the other. You cannot serve God and mammon."* (Matthew 6:24; cf. Luke 16:13). Herein it is also noted that the term "mammon" is a word that is translated from Aramaic to describe wealth and property. Is it not true, therefore, that those who have taken-up the vocation of the religious life have, in fact, denounced the very materialism that has the rest of the world so burdened in debt? Even in the United States, where it is much easier to acquire personal property, there are some who have become so inspired by God to be aligned with the Spirit of His Kingdom which cannot be seen with the naked eye that they have submitted themselves to the grace of His vocational calling. Moreover, it is often by virtue of the prayerful lives of these humble souls that the unabridged origin of our moral and spiritual refinement is conceived.

Those who have accepted the Will of God over the expediency of the world are truly great among us; destined for endeavoring heights in the future that are still quite unknown. Even after seeing life at its near-best in the most wealthy republic between the nations, our young men are still choosing to enter the seminary and become God's servants among His peoples. With all the glitter and glitz of the greatest economy ever known in the history of Creation, these sacrificial souls still put it all behind them in the name of Christian service. Perhaps they, too, can sense the same injustice in our western system of economic prosperity and the potential of our American way of life that often takes us away from the spiritual grace of knowing our Salvation in Jesus Christ better. The Catechism of the Catholic Church states it best, *"The Church...has refused to accept, in the practice of 'capitalism,' individualism and the absolute primacy of the law of the marketplace over human labor. Regulating the economy solely by centralized planning perverts the basis of social bonds; (and) regulating it solely by the law of the marketplace fails social justice, for 'there are many human needs which cannot be satisfied by the market.' Reasonable regulation of the marketplace and economic initiatives, in keeping with a just hierarchy of values and a view to the common good, is to be commended."* (Part Three, Article VII, *The Seventh Commandment*, 2425). This Article of the Catechism speaks explicitly and in direct response to the rules which have been inherently governed by the Sacred Commandment of *"Thou Shalt Not Steal,"* according to the record of both SS. Matthew and Luke. Finally, it is this to which those who have either entered the priestly vocation or are pondering doing so are given to the reasoned explanation that the Kingdom of God cannot be easily emulated by the material world since nearly everyone alive is seeking like-birds of a feather in order to acquire what they can claim for their own nesting-place at the deprivation of others who have no means of self-sufficiency. Jesus Christ deplores such a struggle for supremacy by any mortal man, no matter in what persuasions he may choose to gather; because such becomes the undermining of His unseen manifestation of Truth inside the human heart. In essence, He is asking how we can possibly search for Salvation in an invisible Savior while simultaneously remaining predominantly satisfied with human life the way it is overtly seen. His message is that our lives are only transitory, and our sins are left unmitigated unless they are heaped upon His Crucifixion to be destroyed. Ultimately, this is the very flash of enlightenment that enters the hearts of His priests; and theirs is the mission to teach the rest of us that the domain of all human perfection resides only in following their lead. This is what they pray for during the recitation of their Offices; and our response hinges upon whether we have hearts of receptiveness, or ones of grainy stone. Roman Catholic priests offer the *Seven Canonical Hours* in progressive stages; an example of which is as follows.

Matins	Morning Prayer beginning at midnight or at the break of *dawn*, to pray for world peace and justice around the globe, particularly in war-zones and areas of religious and civil conflict.
Primes	Prayers fixed for the *first* hour of the day, especially to remember the poor, dying, afflicted, abandoned, incarcerated; and the end of abortion, euthanasia, and capital punishment.
Tierce	Prayers fixed for the *third* hour of the day, usually 9:00 a.m., to summon the invocation of the Holy Spirit to respond to the individual petitions of the faithful, particularly for whom the intercession of the Blessed Virgin Mary is beseeched.
Sext	Prayers fixed for the *sixth* hour of the day, taken as noon; for the midday remembrance of the plight of those who do not know God; for atheists, agnostics, reprobates, mortal sinners, and the victims of those who are addicted to sin.
Nones	Prayers fixed for the *ninth* hour of the day, taken as 3:00 p.m., *The Hour of Divine Mercy* to especially remember the poor souls in Purgatory to God for release into the Light of Heaven.
Vespers	Prayers fixed for the early *evening* hours, noted for the higher supplications of purity and chastity for those who may bow to the particular sinfulness that befalls so many mortal souls during the dark hours between dusk and dawn.
Complines	Prayers fixed for the *conclusion* of the day; mostly respected toward offering thanksgiving for prayers answered; for lodging, food, and comfort accorded; and for healing graces throughout the world.

What these sincere devotions mean to humanity is that, while the rest of us are eating our Quaker Oats, reading the morning newspaper, and watching the *Today Show* on television, our priests are imploring the Almighty Father to bring peace to the embattled world. When we arrive at work to garner more profits for our bank accounts and to pay $175.00 for our son's new tennis shoes, those who are wearing the Roman collar are begging Jesus Christ to remember the weak, forsaken, and disenfranchised. When our employer barges into our office during the first half-hour of the morning and approaches our desk to ask if we have completed a report that was due yesterday about the valued price of certain hard commodities in the daily financial markets, the Catholic clergy are praying on bended knee to beseech Jesus Christ to send His Immaculate Mother to infiltrate our hearts and teach us to Love and share the bulk of our wealth with the poor. As we walk into the nearest McDonald's restaurant to order a hot Big Mac, the prayerful souls who have been ordained to advance the Kingdom of God are obediently genuflecting before the Most Blessed Sacrament to bestow His converting presence upon those who still reject Him. Once the afternoon break-bell sounds on our factory floors and their employees slip-out the side door to inhale a cigarette, our Roman Catholic priests are kneeling before the Sacred Altar to offer the Chaplet of The Divine Mercy for the living and the dead. Thereafter, while we are sitting in a basketball stadium somewhere or preparing to watch ER over our satellite receiver, the servants who love our Lord the most are laying prostrate at the apses of our elegant cathedrals to petition God and His Immaculate Mother to restore our interior desire for spiritual awareness and personal discipline. And, when the remaining pins are toppled at the downtown bowling-alley and the competitors take their last sip of beer before driving home in time to catch the final few minutes of their local news, our beloved priests are absorbed in the *complines* of their immanent union with God through His Divine explication of their very beings as they offer their gratitude to Him for having relented in His promise to crush a world that is still so reckless, indifferent, collusive, and corrupt beneath the justified dominance of His Holy Wrath. These are among the wholesome yearnings of priests all over the globe who see the Gates of Paradise within their hearts; who know that only few among us are worthy to receive the sacred gift of Salvation without suffering anything less than painstaking chastisement for the brashness and brutal destruction that our sins have wrought upon Creation. While we are the makers of war, they are God's petitioners for everlasting peace. Ours is a conquest for elusiveness, but theirs is a perfect submission. When all Eternal Truth is fully divulged from

Heaven before the unseasoned masses of the Earth, we shall learn that the real dispensation of plenary indulgence by Jesus Christ upon a humanity that has been so reluctant to accept Him was secretly expedited through the tireless efforts of His Roman Catholic priests.

Henceforth, we should live in the confidence that the interior life of spiritual divinity is founded at the epicenter of the human heart and that our new revival should be discovered in the Domain of the Messianic Son of God whose prophecy was fulfilled, *"...and all shall sing in their festive dance: 'My home is within you.'"* (Psalm 87: 7). This is the essence of our Heavenly Father emanating from the inspirited nature of our conversion to Divine Truth in His Son; which is, beyond any hesitation, the source of all eternal revelation, reciprocity, Wisdom in prayer, dignified guidance, the graceful origin of the Sacraments, and the kindred affection that makes us fall so deeply in love with the souls of other men. It is also the perfect motivation by which we move, breathe, repent and have our inner-being. At the risk of opening myself up to being pummeled by countless letters, land-line facsimiles, email, telegrams, and various other literati; I dare say that most Catholic families in America today are too cowardly to defend the reputation of our good priests in public for fear of not appearing to be sorrowful enough for their mistakes or able to be identified with the trendy movement of criticizing them as do the various formal media outlets and comedians of all stripes; whether they be of the professional or bar-room variety. This, in itself, is a credible threat against the dignity and esteem in which every single one of them is supposed to be held. As a result of this lacking in our laity, could it be true that the same God who created both ants and dinosaurs might allow their minuscule faith and humongous opposition against His Catholic Church to coexist in the same material world; or will those who decline to uphold His clergy go by way of the ancient mastodons? There are still too many uninformed critics and wolves in sheep's clothing living among the faithful; and the Magisterium needs to crack the throttle wide-open in hot pursuit of this neighborhood menace; and, with the threat of excommunication, make them cease and desist from trying to plunder the good reputation of our apostolic clergy. Those who know the Truth best already understand that God is not seeking some mediocre compromise between human sincerity and indignation as we engage our relationship with Heaven through organized Christianity. Rather, He is calling for a protracted assault against sin and impurity, with nothing-less than our most extreme purposefulness in ensuring that the principles of His Messianic Doctrine are precisely fulfilled. The whole idea of contrasting physical agony and victorious ecstasy may be alright for promoting the ABC Wide World of Sports program, but daily life is more commonplace than that; composed mostly of ordinary struggles in which we ultimately see either success or defeat as the final result. There are very few crescendoes which have become the milestones and dividing lines in history for most casual lives, unless we count the horrific tragedies which have brought us all to bow our heads in shame for the ruthless decadence of modern America. Rarely have any of us been allowed to become knotty activists in some great political dynasty, superstars on a stage, or those who are chosen to be launched to the moon in rocket-powered spaceships. For the most part, our memories are peppered with personal crises, soul-wrenching losses, the parting of our loved-ones, bouts with illness, emotional distress, financial hardship, spiritual deprivation, and physical abuse. If we look into the future only with incredulous eyes, it is probably by force of habit because our spirits have already been bludgeoned and broken by the scars inflicted through the travails of the past. With what new hope can we anticipate better things to come? By remaining true to our Christian faith, standing shoulder-to-shoulder against the enemies of the Church, and praying like wildfire that Jesus will soon deliver us from the modern-day facade of erotic delusion that is being paraded before us by Satan's riotous convicts and villainous hellions.

It would seem awfully barbaric and hypocritical that we, too, might choose to float the theme of charitable forgiveness in our writings and speeches to our friends and the media at the same time we are calling for exposing the sins of our estranged family members and clergy before the hordes of tabloid-mongers on the downtown square. The inferior qualities of our own attributes will not sustain us if our lives should be laid-bare before Creation in a likewise manner. The entire of humanity should turn, instead, to God for mutual absolution and unqualified patience while we are growing our individual compassion. Such Love and hope are our two pillars of earthly justice; the "Saints Peter and Paul" of the unseen interior of Christianity inside our souls; the former is the key to comprehending the essence of Heaven, and the latter is the inspiration we need for our hearts and outward lives to move forward with hawthorn-beauty to be diverted completely away from persecuting our faithful brethren so as to facilitate their journey to Eternal Salvation. We must have these two catechetical feet planted firmly in the Truth if we expect to stand fully upright before the rest of the world as the descendants of a grace-filled concordance of timely divinity in Jesus. The sacred unity of all Christians is ultimately dependent upon this very kind of confident stature. And, what about those who decline our request? It seems awfully shameful that many adversaries of the Church are forced to discover the hard way that we have been telling them the truth all along by waiting until they pass into the annals of history through their own natural deaths and see it for themselves. They should have realized that there is a "first" and a "last" for everything; as someone had to hit a baseball over the fence in a nondescript ballpark to the light of the moon somewhere and invent the first home run. Likewise, there has been only one undergraduate on Earth to have been the first to be awarded a college degree. And, probably in the plains of Oklahoma, God created the very first vortex of a tornado; and He will surely preside over the last of all of these. Someday, the final giddy bachelor will walk through the exit of a commencement convocation; the towering floodlights will fade-to-black at Yankee Stadium, and humanity will stand alone with his collective hands drooping, wondering why most everything we ever did had little, if anything, to do with our preparation for being judged by every man's Hero: Jesus Christ. As the end of the course of human events rapidly approaches, it is almost like waiting for the storm-clouds to pass that have chased us all indoors, although it is not a woeful prospect for the millions who have been praying in sorrow and distress for relief from their pain.

      The only perpetual beginning and permanent ending to all mortal history is the *Alpha* and the *Omega*, the first and last; for Christ is the parametric finisher to His Creation under whose muscat arbors we satisfy our curiosity as to whether God ever started "somewhere" in the universe to manifest the restoration of the Earth while appealing to His own conscience by rescuing us who inhabit it from among the dead. Believe it or not, He has given a genetic composition to the entire facility of our supernatural progression toward perfection under the guidance of the Cross; not one that can be detected by thin glass slides and magnifying lenses in a laboratory somewhere, but an identifiable panacea of Truth which is intrinsic to every man, in its purest form; and is the fruit of the distillation of our souls through our encounter with the Sacred Mysteries of the Life, Death, and Resurrection of Jesus Christ. We are distinguished as being among the redeemed through the architecture of His sacrificial Love and the transfer of our volitional concession into the flames of His Most Sacred Heart; for therein, we are tested, tempered, and indoctrinated to exist at the precise center of Our Lord's Eternal Being. So, when we are lauding Him through the first of the Canonical Hours by chanting our morning *Te Deum*, we are essentially renewing the tendency of our spirits to remain united to His Will for yet another day. It is quite obvious that few of us know what moment in time will be our last; but it is sufficient to affirm that it would become the best of all possible consequences to make it an occasion that is adorned by our most tenable faith. If we were able to elongate the reach of our eardrums past the point of death, we might be able to hear the voice of the very Adam from whom we inherited our sinful nature proclaiming at the top of his lungs that even *he* would have it no other way. Jesus can make any event in Creation retroactive to its origin for the purpose of amending its course; and there is no doubt that we can retrieve the innocence we lost when Adam and Eve took that fateful bite. Their savoring of such error was not even slightly the nutriment they thought it would be; and there are more than a few striking similarities between their disobedience to God in the Garden of Eden and how we are allowing our lives to unfold today. It was not until Christ dispensed the Fruits from the Cross that humanity even came close to becoming fit for the consumption of God's intermediary Grace which thereafter begot the swift reversal of our spiritual emaciation and began the inexorable collision between human pride and Divine Truth. And, as for Our Lord's response to the weaknesses of His Church, Jesus is going to return to the Earth with a sword in His hands to destroy our haughty impurity alright; but we will all be very surprised when He bypasses the penitent priests whom He has already forgiven through the Sacrament of Confession and drives the saber of His Holy Wrath deeply into the calcified hearts of the rest of us; we who have created, financed, marketed, and displayed His Crucifixion on the Cross inside a massive container of urine and those who have depicted an image of His Immaculate Mother, the Blessed Virgin Mary, with feces smeared all over Her face.

It makes no sense for us to deny that God will hold us responsible as the Mystical Body of His Church for allowing the desecration of His Sacred icons to continue. He requires humanity to see the hypocrisy in splattering the faults of our priests across the printed medium and the electronic airways, when these very same ordained servants tell us in the privacy of a confessional that our sins are forgiven by God, Himself; and that we should expunge them from our memories. We have forgotten that it is only by our wilful devotion to Him that He knows that we love Him in return. Indeed, is it not more romantic for us to receive the voluntary love of someone else when it is a product of their own innate desire, and not because they are forced to feign it for fear of violating our higher rank or superior dominion over them? Jesus Christ would not covet even a morsel of our love if it is not a Divine engagement that we equally crave to receive from Him. God did not slip any leaves of hemlock into His Cup of Eternal Salvation to sedate us into seeking our spiritual purification in Him; but He offers us, instead, the sobering mortification of Jesus Crucified to wake us from our mortal sleep. We are given a human "will" which is capable of choosing our destiny beside the Almighty Father and the Paradisial Court with expiatory spontaneity, and with all the acuteness of our premeditated consent. The ball is now in our court because we are drawn in conscience and faith to remain true to *ourselves* in accepting Salvation in Christ, a decision that is a product of our internal meditation and the maintaining of a perpetual oratory with God, in all of His magisterial power. As for His Catholic priests; indeed, for the laity too, the Church gives us the formal *Liturgy of the Hours* as a means of sanctifying our grace to remain loyal to Jesus in conjunction with our attendance at daily Mass. It is found in the Roman Catechism, Part Two, Chapter Two, Article I.

1174   *"The mystery of Christ, His Incarnation and Passover, which we celebrate in the Eucharist especially at the Sunday assembly, permeates and transfigures the time of each day through the celebration of the Liturgy of the Hours—The Divine Office. This celebration, faithful to the apostolic exhortations to 'pray constantly,' is so devised that the whole course of the day and night is made holy by the praise of God. In this public prayer of the Church, the faithful (clergy, religious, and lay people) exercise the royal priesthood of the baptized. Celebrated in the form approved by the Church, the Liturgy of the Hours is truly the voice of the Bride herself addressed to her Bridegroom. It is the very prayer which Christ, Himself, together with His Body, addresses to the Father."*

1176   *"The celebration of the Liturgy of the Hours demands not only harmonizing the voice with the praying heart, but also a deeper understanding of the liturgy and of the Bible, especially of the Psalms."*

1177   *"The hymns and litanies of the Liturgy of the Hours integrate the prayer of the Psalms into the age of the Church, expressing the symbolism of the time of day, the liturgical season, or the feast being celebrated. Moreover, the reading from the Word of God at each hour...and readings from the Fathers and spiritual masters at certain Hours, reveal more deeply the meaning of the mystery being celebrated, assist in understanding the Psalms, and prepare for silent prayer. The 'lectio divina,' where the Word of God is so read and meditated that it becomes prayer, is thus rooted in the liturgical celebration."*

1178   *"The Liturgy of the Hours, which is like an extension of the Eucharistic celebration, does not exclude, but rather in a complementary way, calls forth the various devotions of the People of God, especially adoration and worship of the Blessed Sacrament."*

Chapter V
We Remember How You Loved Us

"The priest, indeed, is the minister of God, using the Word of God, and by the command and institution of God; but God Himself is there, the principle Author and invisible worker, to Whom is subject all that He Wills, and to whose command everything is obedient...For this is not due to any merits of men that a man should consecrate and handle the Sacrament of Christ...Great is this Mystery, and great the dignity of priests, to whom that is given which is not granted to angels."

Thomas 'a Kempis
My Imitation of Christ
Book IV, Chapter 5

I was peering out the window of my bedroom before sitting-down at my desk to pen this chapter in early May 2002. The obvious signs of Spring were there; the tulips and violets were abloom in my neighbor's yard alongside the broadleaves and pesky dandelions, the peonies were opening on their stems, infant buds were blowing on the sycamores in the breezes over the rooftops of our homes, and the towering cottonwood trees were bustling with squirrels, robins, and gray turtle doves. My house is situated near Oak Ridge Cemetery in Springfield, Illinois where our "Humble Servant" Abraham Lincoln is buried, along with the American poet Vachel Lindsay, former governor Big John Tanner, and the corpses of a host of other people who hardly anyone remembers anymore. Our environment seems to be replete with such contradictions; what with the arrival of a fresh hope in a new season amidst the interred remains of our tragic past. We all manage to continue our daily lives, however; as we ultimately have no choice. And, just when I was pondering how beautiful the world could be if only we would imitate the quiet excellence of Nature, I picked-up the newspaper and began to read about the tragic distractions that keep us all from getting there. As I continued my cursory look at the morning news, I saw that the United States was cringing in shame for having accidently killed four Canadian servicemen in mid-April when a warplane from my hometown dropped a 500-pound bomb on them during a live-fire training exercise near Kandahar, Afghanistan. We were harshly reminded as a result of this event that our troops were there together to prosecute a war against the Taliban and al-Qaida forces for the terrorist attacks in New York and Washington, D.C. on September 11, 2001.

Adjacent headlines offered various reflections about the recession of our nation's economy, the Chernobyl nuclear explosion in the former Soviet Union in April 1986, the historical aftermath of the killing of John Wilkes Booth by federal troops in 1865, a look-back at the U.S. having exploded a one-megaton "boxcar" nuclear device beneath the Nevada desert in 1968, the incarceration and scattering of the American hostages inside Iran in 1980, the recent murder of a gas-station attendant just four-blocks from my front door, and the ongoing skirmishes between Israel and the Palestinians in the Middle East.

It did not take me very long to decide that it would be better for me to put down the paper and refocus my attention upon the warbling birds and lofty clouds outside. I suppose it might be a trite interrogatory by now for most of us, but all I could think-of that morning was the same question that little children have about certain confusing issues they cannot seem to understand: why? From what circumstances have the United States and the rest of the world allowed our level of human interaction and dereliction to reach such catastrophic heights? Is mortal sin so integrated into our international psyche that we are forced to believe that its existence is all-but inevitable? Should we not revert our attention back to the simplicity of life we saw in those quaint episodes of Bonanza and Andy Griffith on TV when we were still sitting like olive-plants around our parents' dinner tables everyday? Indeed, the spirit of our conscience is designed to return us there soon; and nearly everyone alive has an internal reminiscence already begging to be revealed. Only the memories of our youthful rendezvous with God will suffice for connecting us to the child-like fragrances of the strength we garner from the past. If it is true that we live what we learn as youngsters, then the world should not make heroes of its national leaders anymore; or its scientists, doctors, or entertainers; but only those who have taken our hearts closest to Heaven. This is the essential reason why it is much more mandatory than just appropriate for us to recall the legacies of our foregone clergy. If we are holy, it is because they taught us to be. If we yearn to see Paradise while the rest of the globe agonizes in tyranny, they are the benefactors who seeded it in us. I have chosen to remember a few of them here; not for the purpose of hiding their memories in some elegy or behind a gloomy epitaph in a rural cemetery, but for admiring the vision of history, itself, for allowing them to become a fashion of its own stately architecture. There are hundreds-of-thousands who have come and gone by now; all of whom belong to the endless Eternity and preeminent Love of our Triune God.

Reverend Father Chester Fabisiak, S.J.
The Princely Confessor
1911 - 1996

On the 11th of June 1911, a humble servant of Almighty God was born to humankind in Poznan, Poland who would live nearly nine decades to the benison of all the world, a blessing to the entire mass of exiled sinners, and a benign spiritual hero to the United States. The biography from which I have written about Father Chester was inscribed on the reverse side of a Card of Memoriam that was dispensed during his funeral at the Blessed Sacrament Church in Springfield, Illinois. He was Baptized into Christ only seven days after his birth; he entered the Society of Jesus in August 1927, and was ordained a priest on June 18, 1939. What our Dear Lord would ask of this pious little man before his life was ended would take the breath of a less humble soul, for he was taken prisoner by the SS commandoes during World War II only three months later, where he was forced to spend nearly six years inside the "living hell" that was to become known as the infamous Dachau concentration camp. I had the opportunity to speak with Father Chester about the agony he suffered there, although he was rather reticent to go into detail about it. After his liberation from Dachau on April 29, 1945 by Allied forces, he served as a missionary in Ecuador and Argentina, South America until 1966; whereupon he was transferred to service in New York, Dearborn, Detroit; and the cities of Springfield, Taylorville, New Berlin, and Quincy in Illinois. Father Chester was also briefly assigned to the St. Ignatius parish, Santa Cruz, Bolivia in 1978. And, just like a storybook-ending would have it, he became a naturalized citizen of the United States on September 23, 1974, precisely 35 years to-the-day after he was first taken prisoner in WWII. We remember from our Civics classes here in America that the testimony of a person who is sworn under oath in a matter before the courts is recorded by a stenographer; the conclusion of which is sealed with the customary "...the deponent further sayeth not." Let me assure you that the witness which was given by Father Chester Fabisiak on behalf of Jesus Christ will live forever past the end of the ages, high and above the Firmament of Truth and Justice, and is still ringing with clarity across the billions of precipices of universes unknown. He was prompt to tell me that no man is beyond Salvation and, even in all the darkness of his memories, he reminded me that Christ is now rightfully admonishing each of us that there are millions of souls alive on the Earth today who know not what they are doing against His Kingdom of Divine Love. He always predicated his assurance about this upon my own vision of the way the world ought to be, knowing in his heart that I, too, wore the interior callouses upon my spirit that are intrinsic to everyone. Although his English was a bit broken and often difficult to understand; especially in his later years, Father Chester had absolutely no problem whatsoever in calling his faithful flock to the higher dimensions of human forgiveness, charity, servitude, responsibility, and Love. I once sponsored a catechumen into the Roman Catholic faith in 1994 during the RCIA program at the Blessed Sacrament Church in Springfield, where Father Chester spoke to the group during one of the evening presentations. He was only about five-feet, six-inches tall, but the roof above and the sky overhead could not contain the homiletics of this giant Catholic priest. One might have thought that Jesus Christ, Himself, had again been reincarnated in a frail eighty-year-old man, standing before us to proclaim that His Kingdom literally cannot be very far beyond the grasp of our immediate senses.

Father Fabisiak had been in residence at the Blessed Sacrament Church in Springfield since mid-1981 before I met him about ten years thereafter. I cannot remember him ever saying any of the regular Sunday morning Masses after 1994, unless I was not present at the time, because the church was blessed to have had a sufficient number of parochial vicars, along with their pastors, to offer the Liturgy of the Holy Eucharist; so it was probably not necessary to call upon him anyway. There is no doubt that his advanced age might have had something to do with it. He was prone to walk around the neighborhood of South Walnut and Laurel streets after dark by himself, reciting the Sacred Mysteries of the Most Holy Rosary along the way. And, believe me, if there had been a turtle or a snail walking alongside him, they would have had to slow down to keep from running too far ahead. Father Chester was also known for listening quite intensely to the Holy Spirit as he asked God for the preservation, healing, protection, and sanctification of humankind. One night, during one of his evening strolls, he was urged by the Divine nature of his obedience to Jesus to stop at a house where he had been completely unexpected to arrive, knock on the front door, and tell the unsuspecting occupant that he had come to hear their confession. Imagine being the resident who was probably grieving at that very moment about the burdens of their sins. Indeed, the peace and grace which flowed from the Most Sacred Heart of Jesus was supernaturally present in the dispensation of His absolution through the Sacrament of Reconciliation as it was administered by Father Fabisiak. As one of my personal confessors, I have this sacred knowledge etched quite lovingly and permanently in the confines of my soul. Many were the times when I would step most contritely into the confessional, take a seat before this Christian legend, ask for his understanding in my weaknesses, and listen while he played the entire orchestration of mortal repentance through the genius of his words, the pity in his eyes, the Wisdom of his advice, and the bestowing of the very pardon from God that my soul needed at the time.

Before he died on the Feast of the Immaculate Conception of the Blessed Virgin Mary in 1996, I came to know Father Chester as a diplomat for the spiritual genuflection of all humankind before Heaven, a warrior in the fight against the American culture of death, and a compliant witness to the Will of God for our contemporary age. There was no one on Earth who was more devoted to our Holy Mother; and his innocence authenticated his commission from his station under Her protective Mantle. When once asked the question whether he thought that the Holy Sacrifice of the Mass was purely a reflection of Christ's Crucifixion, he unabashedly proclaimed that the Holy Mass is the concurrent and original consortium of The Last Supper and the Crucifixion of Jesus on the Cross brought through time by the power of God in Heaven to rest upon the Altar of Sacrifice. Just as our Baptism is the preeminent grace to the cleansing of our souls in the Blood of Christ, the Holy Sacrifice of the Mass is our participation in the one and only Crucifixion in preparation for our reunion with Him on the day we die. Father Chester was also very adamant in confirming that the Sacrament of Penance is our instrument for keeping our Baptismal Gown clean from stain and, in turn, our souls purified before our Final Redemption across the chasm of the lingering ages and into the bounty of Everlasting Life. When asked how someone knows that we are washed in the Blood of Jesus when we cannot see or feel it, his response was that the human "will" allows our soul to be set free from sin inside the Sacrifice of Jesus on the Cross by which we are bathed. Thereafter, we fall asleep in Christ by submersion in His Sacred Blood, and are raised from mortal death by virtue of His own Resurrection from the Sepulcher. Father Fabisiak preached, taught, and lived these articles of Truth as his second nature while breathing-in the facility of a sanctified life. He walked in a manner of grace and accord with the Eternal Dominion of God because his soul reflected His Love to near-perfection while he lived among us here on Earth. Those who spoke so profoundly about him at the concelebration of his funeral Mass, including then-Bishop Daniel Leo Ryan, were fond to recall Father Chester as a man of unequivocal suffering and sacrifice to rival the greatest of the Saints. For his undying Love, gentleness, servitude, patience, and morality, we shall long remember him as a friend and hero of Christian piety. God, Himself, would have it no other way; for the facets of this humble priest's holiness have forever more clearly defined our pathway to Paradise.

Saint Jean-Marie-Baptiste Vianney
Patron of Priests
1786 - 1859

It is by virtue of this indelible Saint that the French title *cure`*, which means "parish priest," has been forever engraved into the history of all Christendom. His legacy is more than quite the reason why we mortals of the Earth are urged to call upon the intercession of the Communion of Saints in our times of trouble; especially for those who are serving religious vocations. St. John Vianney spent the final forty-years of his life ministering to the Village of Ars, which is situated about thirty kilometers from Lyons, France. He was surnamed the *Cure`d'Ars* for having transformed a remote plateau of clay and stagnant waters into an international icon of Catholic Christianity; where his body was entombed upon his death on August 4, 1859 and exhumed 45 years later in June 1904, and later transferred intact into *The Holy Shrine of the Cure`d'Ars*. He was canonized a Saint of the Catholic Church on the Feast of Pentecost, May 31, 1925 by Pope Pius XI, after two miraculous healings attributed to his direct intercession had been recorded before his Beatification ceremonies during the Pontifical reign of Pius X, who declared him to be the "...patron of all parish priests of France" in 1905; and two additional miracles which occurred shortly thereafter that were subjected to the ordinary scrutinies under the Pontificate of Benedict XV in 1920. Pius XI thereupon also named him to be the Patron of Parish Priests of all the world. It is widely known through the purview of public domain that St. John Vianney was an articulate speaker, but lacking in the quantitative intelligence to place him at the fore of his peers. In fact, he "deplored" the idea of formal classroom learning; unsure as to its value before the greater Kingdom of human Redemption in the Crucifixion of Jesus Christ. He became interested in the priesthood at a young age and began his studies at Ecully under Abbe` Balley, receiving his first tonsure when he entered the seminary at Lyons in 1813, and was ordained a priest in 1815 through the direct assistance of Abbe` Balley upon the revelation that his faith and piety eclipsed the lacking in his fundamental education. He was thereafter appointed the Cure` of Ars in 1818, where he spent the remainder of his mortal years. Indeed, it was through his guidance, service, perseverence, and spirituality that he transformed an impoverished village into one of the most holy places on the face of the Earth, and garnered himself the homage of the whole of France, millions of Catholics around the globe, and the Hierarchy of the Apostolic Church. What would a man who had so little respect for the formalities of civics and the fluency of Latin be able to accomplish in a terrain of such rustic abandon? The answer to this question is the reason I have placed him in my book. He met Christ's opposition head-on, with determination and invincible love; discipline, a voracious curiosity, the embodiment of self-denial, laborious service (he often spent fifteen hours a day in the confessional to administer the Rite of Reconciliation to his faithful flock), contemplative prayer, and a uniquely deep devotion to the Blessed Virgin Mary. If he passed anyone on the streets of the Village of Ars who was making small-talk about the weather or rumoring about the lives of other men, he would stop and chastise them, reminding them of their own transgressions; often miraculously being able to recount their unconfessed sins with articulate detail and, thereafter, recommending them to receive the Sacrament of Penance before dusk fell on that very night. To others, he would say that the great Francis of Assisi, who had died 600 years before, would descend from Heaven, himself, and help Vianney expunge the evils from their souls like a whiplash in the night if he chose to summon such vast miraculous power. This approach yielded Father Vianney a large number of critics and detractors, most of whom had little in common with his life of piousness or dedication to the faith of many in the Church. Never once was anyone able to prove any of the libelous accusations or falsehoods that were lodged against him. He commissioned a shrine to Saint Philomena, the child whose posthumous apostolate was authorized by Pope Gregory XVI in 1837; whereupon Father Vianney began a shelter for young girls in Ars which quickly grew into a large homeless shelter for countless orphans.

There can be no overstating Saint John Vianney's unbridled disdain for the ranting palavers of the secular world. He might have been called into higher service by the Church Hierarchy as his years progressed, but his superiors were somewhat hesitant because they were unsure when he was likely to go on another tirade against the hypocrisy of certain secular men or against the materialism that was such an enemy of their faith. The main burden that he bore for the latter half of his life, however, was the habitual attacks upon him by the evil of Satan. There are stories aplenty about how he was forced into mental darkness, physical agony, and spiritual anguish, but Vianney was reluctant to advance a great deal of facts surrounding them because he did not want anyone in his midst to pity him while he continued to suffer gladly for Christ. The main contention of those who opposed him was that he was quite socially estranged, reprehensibly uneducated, and psychologically eccentric; but this saintly gentlemen was "crazy like a fox."

He knew precisely what needed to be done to nudge humanity from its bubbled-station, high atop the pillars of indifference and frivolity. If anyone would wish to come to know Saint John Vianney during his mortal life, they would be required to approach him through the properties of the heart: honesty, candor, uprightness, fairness, truthfulness, virtuosity, and chastity. It was not that he feared having his feelings hurt or that he saw an ulterior motivation to interacting with others, but his soul was actually capable of discerning where Satan was concealed in the thoughts and actions of those around him, and where evil struck in various attacks of vengeance because of the countless souls he was winning for Christ. One such accounting is recorded in the book, *The Cure'd'Ars*, by Father Francis Trochu (Burns, Oates, & Washbourne, London, 1927). In Chapter XI therein, entitled "The Cure'd'Ars and the Devil," an event is retold from the morning of February 23 or 24, 1857, *"...the saint had started hearing confessions at an unusually early hour by reason of the great crowds assembled in the church, where the Blessed Sacrament was exposed. A little before seven o'clock, some persons were passing by the presbytery when they noticed a fire in M. Vianney's room. He was promptly informed, just as he was about to leave his confessional to say Mass. 'It would seem, Father, that your room is on fire!' He just handed the key to those who had brought the information, so that they might put-out the flames, and without any excitement he simply said: 'The villainous grappin! He could not catch the bird, so he burns the cage.' He left the church, however, and passed into his courtyard, where he met with the men who, at that very moment, were carrying out of the house the smoking remains of his poor bed. He asked no questions, went back to the church, and once more entered into the sacristy. As may be imagined, some commotion had been caused among the women penitents who crowded the nave of the church...A watchful sacristan thought that perhaps the saint was yet unaware of the cause of the excitement. 'M. le Cure', it is your bed that has been burnt.' 'Ah!' was all he said, in a tone of utter indifference, then calm, as he always was, he went to say his Mass. A young missionary...rushed into the room at the first signal of alarm and at once noticed the mysterious character of the fire. 'The bed, the tester, the curtains of the bed, and everything near—everything had been consumed. The fire had only halted in front of the reliquary of St. Philomena, which had been placed on a chest of drawers. From that point, it had drawn a line from top to bottom with geometrical accuracy, destroying everything on this side of the holy relic and sparing all on the other. As the fire had started without cause, so it died-out in a like manner, and it is very remarkable, and in some ways truly miraculous, that the flames had not spread from the heavy serge hangings to the floor of the upper storey, which was very low, old, and very dry,* *and which would have blazed like straw. At noon, when M. le Cure` came to see me…we spoke of the event. I told him that it was universally looked-upon as a bad joke of the devil, and I asked him whether he really thought that the evil one had had something to do with it. He replied very positively and with the greatest composure: ' Oh! My friend, that is plain enough! He (the devil) is angry; that is a good sign; we shall see many sinners.' As a matter of fact, there followed an extraordinary influx of people into Ars, which lasted for several days.*" (Chapter. XI ff.)

It is quite obvious that Satan was both redundant and relentless in his attacks upon Father Vianney, as he has been throughout the centuries against many in his likeness, in an effort to distract our holy priests from accomplishing their apostolic missions by frightening them into seeking quarters farther from grace. The book from which the above-cited passage is taken was translated by Dom Ernest Graf, OSB, of St. Mary's Abbey in Buckfast; and we are allowed to see most accurately the cool temperament through which Father Vianney came to expect the revenge of Satan against his service and anyone else who was converting souls to Christianity. This must be regarded as a lesson for the rest of us, too. When we are burdened by the onslaught of the physical world against our piety, or when our hearts feel pelted by the vileness of atheists and anti-Christians, the Holy Spirit will remind us that a great legacy has been left before us in the likes of Saint John Vianney, Blessed Father Francesco Pio, Saint Francis of Assisi, Saint Joan of Arc, and scores of others who were forced to do battle against the very pain and agony that was endured by Christ during His Passion and Crucifixion on Good Friday. The numerous attacks of evil against Father Vianney bore witness to the fact that every helpless sinner can suffer in the image of our Divine Lord when we choose to attest to His Holy Gospel and walk where His feet once tread. Although we may never gain such notoriety as to have someone record the history of our lives in a million-seller biography, God knows our every kind act of goodness in His Name that we shall ever effect. He is fully aware of the perils surrounding us everyday, and the stumbling blocks that His sworn enemies from Hell are placing in our path. We dare not take the force of Satan for granted, lest we inadvertently fall victim into his traps; but there is no need to fear him if we confirm the assurance of our power of Love in the Cross of Mount Calvary. The Blood of Jesus Christ is the origin of final death to all evil; and this is what gave Father Vianney the composure to scoff at such assaults against his life. And, so there will be no confusion: every Saint before us has fought against the devil by praying more deeply, soliciting the conversion of sinners more widely, and heaping the crosses of the weak upon their own backs. Such has been the wondrous gift to humanity of the priests and religious who have adorned the Earth with their mortal lives. As has been said about Father Vianney, himself; they are the candle-lighters of Divine Truth for all the world; catechizing children, admonishing agnostics, fighting impurity, erecting cathedrals, liberating the imprisoned, glorifying the Cross, consecrating the Blessed Sacrament, filling omissions, indulging the weak, comforting the grieving, rescuing the forsaken, edifying misguided youths, instructing the ignorant, and refining their own humility. I highly recommend that all Christians read *The Cure`d'Ars*, by Father Francis Trochu, which is also available from TAN Books and Publishers in Rockford, Illinois. One can easily detect the innate intuitions, accurate predictions, and inexplicable miracles which flourished through St. John Vianney's life and eternal rest beyond the heights of Paradise. As told by a penitent in Father Trochu's book, "...*when I came into this district, I heard so much about that priest that I wished to see for myself. I had no intention of going to confession; I just wanted to gain information. Well, I was so struck by the man's appearance that I conceived a desire to speak to him. I entered the sacristy and he bade me kneel down in his confessional. 'My friend,' he asked, 'how long is it since you were at confession?' 'Ah! It is such a long time, Father, that I cannot remember.' 'Examine yourself well; is it twenty-eight years?' 'Twenty-eight years? Twenty-eight years? Yes, that is it.' 'And, you did not receive Holy Communion; you only had absolution.' That was also correct. Upon this, I felt a quickening of my faith, and so lively did it become that I believe I made a very good confession, and I promised God never again to give-up my faith.*" (Chapter XXVI, ff.) In gratitude and remembrance of the consoling holiness of Saint Jean-Marie-Baptiste Vianney, never again shall we ever be tempted to surrender the hustings upon which our Christian evangelization is now proudly stationed or relinquish the power we own in summoning the intercession of all the Saints and Martyrs who are brandishing the Love of God with the grace and elegance of Ancient Kings.

Reverend Father Joseph Timothy Murray
Diocesan Pastor
1913 - 1991

If we listened quietly enough to the eternal breezes whirling across the rural plains of the Diocese of Springfield in Illinois, we would probably still be able to hear the impish chuckling of one of the most debonair and spiritually dynamic priests to ever take the oath in upholding the dignity of the religious vocation. Father Joseph Murray was all-in-everything to those who knew him well. Born in March 1913, he was graduated and ordained a Roman Catholic priest in 1939 and served briefly at the parish of Grafton before being assigned post-graduate studies at the Catholic University of America in Washington, D.C., earning the M.A. degree. Upon his return from the east coast, he became an assistant superintendent of Catholic Schools in Springfield, and later appointed the position of Superintendent for Catholic Education in 1943. Father Murray worked among quite a holy and elite group of Diocesan Directors under then-Bishop Reverend William Aloysius O'Connor, D.D. and the Metropolitan of the five suffragan Illinois dioceses, His Eminence Samuel Cardinal Stritch, Archbishop of Chicago. Their revered legacy is quite a tribute to their dedication of obedience and adherence to the Divine Virtues of the Catholic faith. Many people will recall Father Murray's associates when he served as Director of Education; including The Very Reverend Monsignor William J. Cassin at the Office of Catholic Charities, Fr. Michael O. Driscoll who served in the Chancery and was later elevated to the stature of monsignor, Fr. James Haggerty who was then Director for the Propagation of the Faith, Fr. Raymond F. O'Connor at the Office of CYO, and the Very Reverend Monsignor Jesse L. Gatton who was Director of Catholic Hospitals for the Diocese. Father Murray concurrently taught religion, history, and ethics at Ursuline Academy and Springfield Junior College beginning in 1944 while he served on the Board of Diocesan Directors. Even in all of this, in 1958, a 45-year-old Father Joseph Murray wished to return to service among the peoples in the local parishes because his heart was closest to those who mourned, the diseased and the poor; and young adults who were seeking to begin the adventures of life anew and start a family together. He was appointed pastor of St. Michael's Catholic Church in Sigel, Illinois that year, was transferred to Our Lady of Lourdes in Decatur until 1966, became pastor at St. Mary's parish in Marshall in 1968, moved to St. Louis Catholic Church in Nokomis in 1969, and served the final leg of his long priesthood by relocating to St. Augustine Church in Ashland in early

1977, where he was also assigned to the mission Church of the Visitation in Alexander. For the record, he later relinquished service at Alexander due to his advanced age, but remained as pastor and administrator of the small Ashland parish before announcing his retirement after offering the Holy Sacrifice of the Mass on Sunday, March 10, 1991. We shall remember that day not only because it would portend the closure of his fourteen-years service to St. Augustine Church in which I was reared from my infancy, but also because Father left town after Mass that day, got in his Ford Taurus automobile, and traveled twelve miles west to the City of Virginia, Illinois, where he had driven practically every Sunday since he had arrived in Ashland, to have lunch with his friends at a small restaurant there. But, this time, after exiting the highway as usual, he began to travel the blacktop road that would take him into the downtown business district. Suddenly, his car veered to the right, impacted a fence-line that surrounded a horse corral, and one of the large wooden beams pierced his windshield and glanced-off of his face, fracturing his neck in the process. He was not killed instantly, but was taken to St. John's Hospital in Springfield, where he lived just six days thereafter.

None of us could allow the tragic way that Father Murray died to overshadow our memories of his life of kindness, his affable demeanor, and his love for little children. In all his formal education, positions of high rank and authority in the Springfield Diocese, as professor of history and religion, and all the rest; he never lost sight of his own youthful past when he would run and play around the bushes in the courtyard of the Illinois State Capitol. His heart could not be defeated, even if he would have ever tried to do it on his own, for it could not fail; as this man loved humanity with the affection of the Angels, themselves. He carried food to the poor when he was nearly unable to walk on his own. He visited prison inmates, many of whom he had never met before, to pray with them and offer the simplicity of his inspiration as their new hope for tomorrow. The power of his vocation shined almost blindingly-beautiful during the High Feasts of Our Lord's Nativity in December, the Paschal Celebration of Easter, and the Candlemas observation of the Presentation of Jesus in the bosom of the Blessed Virgin Mary on February 2nd every year. He prayed incessantly for global peace, especially in Northern Ireland; and his petitions rallied the entire forces of God's Creation for the aiding of the poor souls in Purgatory, for the unborn innocents, and those who were oppressed in places that only few among us ever heard of. Father was a vibrant man in his early days, but the years I knew him after he turned 65 saw him tanning-back a little in his rife criticism of the secular world that had previously been much in the lineage of St. John Vianney.

Indeed, he knew the power of the Sacraments in which we were all participating quite well. I once approached him aside one day and asked him to briefly ponder the impact upon the world that the Holy Eucharist brings to humanity. His answer was an appropriate one for a man of such Light and Truth; telling me that at the moment a priest holds the gifts before him and consecrates the bread into the Body, Blood, Soul, and Divinity of Jesus Christ upon the Altar of Sacrifice; the very Host in his hands becomes a perfect place in Creation through the Divine Physical Presence of the Son of God. I look back now through the many years when I lived in the Village of Ashland, and I can see with beatific hindsight that our little town of 1,200 souls was overwhelmingly blessed to have harbored the Holy Eucharist in our midst under the intercession of St. Augustine, and through the pious service of priests like Father Murray.

He ran the course of human endeavor with us there; baptizing our newborns, presiding over our marriages, burying our deceased, hearing our confessions, admonishing our laxity and; most of all, crying with us when we were in pain, walking at our side when we were left alone, hailing the victories of our tiny high school, grieving with us in our personal losses, and celebrating with us when the Lord had accorded us a moment to cheer. His jesting was about as humorous as his punch-lines because his voice always broke into a chuckle at the thought of what he was about to say next; and he would giggle uncontrollably while trying to enunciate the remaining syllables of a joke. The entire Diocese of Springfield was happy because Father Murray was happy; even in the face of the wars in which our country was engaged; he would embrace the survivors of their victims and remind them that the greatest battle of all is for the Kingdom of God; and anyone who had crossed into the bounty of Eternity was assuredly beaming forever-after in the fullness of its grace. His confidence in the promise of Salvation was absolutely unflappable, his trust in the Holy Spirit unwavering, and his hope that humankind of every age would finally learn what *he* knew kept his hope aloft for many solemn years. Even though he was never much moved by miraculous things, such as the supernatural apparitions of Jesus and the Virgin Mary to many seers around the globe, Father Murray was a miracle in himself to the rest of us and our means for comprehending the Most Sacred Heart of Christ in a single mortal man. There are probably a million stories like this one that could be told around the world; and the memory of my friend and Pastor is one which is fond to me. He is buried beside his parents about a mile from my home, and I visit his grave when the weather is not unfair. There is no doubt that his soul is resting peacefully now, as is the entire Corps of Saints who are laughing at his impishness.

From What Then?

When the choir has sung its last anthem,
and the preacher has made his last prayer;
When the people have heard their last sermon,
and the sound has died-out on the air;
When the Bible lies closed on the Altar,
and the pews are all empty of men,
And each one stands facing his record—
and the great Book is opened, What Then?   8

When the actors have played their last drama,
and the mimic has made his last fun;
When the film has flashed its last picture,
and the billboard displayed its last run;
When the crowds seeking pleasure have vanished,
and gone out in the darkness again—
When the trumpet of Ages is sounded,
What Then?   16

When the bugle's call sinks into silence,
and the long marching columns stand still;
When the captain repeats his last orders,
and they've captured the last fort and hill;
When the flag has been hauled from the masthead,
and the wounded afield check-in,
And a world that rejected its Saviour,
is asked for a reason—What Then?   24

—J. Whitfield Green

Section Two
The Monopoly of Truth

Chapter VI
The Holy Sacraments of Salvation

"Today, I have come to understand many of God's mysteries. I have come to know that Holy Communion remains in me until the next Holy Communion. A vivid and clearly felt presence of God continues in my soul. The awareness of this plunges me into deep recollection, without the slightest effort on my part. My heart is a living tabernacle in which the living Host is reserved. I have never sought God in some far-off place, but within myself. It is in the depths of my own being that I commune with my God."

> Sister M. Faustina Kowalska
> From *The Divine Mercy Diary*
> Notebook IV - 1302
> September 29, 1937

Although we are incapable of seeing our own spirit as it lives inside us or extrapolating what it might look like beyond our physical attributes, we know for sure that there must be some type of alcove or vacancy therein which exists when men are born; and that it is this secret passage that God reserves through which to reach us. Whenever we ask Him to fill us up or cry-out in hunger for His graces, it is the hollow atrium of this abandoned palace that we are unwittingly begging Him to reclaim. Jesus left an empty Tomb on the Earth when He rose from the dead almost 2,000 years ago; and through His Divine and mystical purposes, He has placed an exact replica of it inside our hearts; a space for Him to be reposed again in peace; a hallowed chamber of solace, so we can know that His presence inside us is the seed from which our Eternal Salvation must grow. This is why Sister Faustina felt that she was required to encounter Him from within, that only the substance of the spiritual Truth of the unseen Paradise would ever come to greet her there. From what courageous faith must we accept this fact as it has been dispensed through the mortal ages; not just in Sister Faustina's Poland in 1937, but for all the permeating centuries which have heretofore flown both forward and back to the provincial rhythm of God? Jesus Christ reminds us that it springs from a bold and exceptional manifestation called "Divine Love," for without it, there is no life, no future, and nothing of any consequence to pass to the succeeding generations or beyond the shadows of our exiled here-and-now. There is a somewhat monastic counterweight to every living thing that is calling us ever-inward to the exact center of life, despite our innate penchant for exploiting the tangible world. We already know the fate of those who desire only to exercise their lethal knee-jerk slavery to such human curiosity because there are dead hypotheses laying in abandoned streets and in dark ditches all around the globe. If only we could momentarily bring the commotion of the world to a halt, we would begin to comprehend, at the very least, that the greater expansion of our purpose in life can be neither contained nor commanded from atop the coattails of our mutual grudges or the calculation of our industrial works. The great American poet John Robinson Jeffers (1887-1962) suggested that humanity should fall in love *outward*, i.e., our affection for God must become, as Sister Faustina prescribed, a function of Jesus Christ growing inside humankind by virtue of the instrumental vowing of our conscience toward echoing His Truth from within that very same invisible canyon of sublime opportunity which lives at the center of our souls.

Every Saint who ever anticipated their Salvation repeated this strain for the maturation of their infant faith to ensure the procession of God's Divine intervention in their every fashion of life. Such trust is the identical Truth that brought SS. Francis and Augustine to acknowledge that their self-mortification must have been the only path to eternal subsistence with Christ in Heaven because no sinner in their midst could wield His sense of perfection as they had come to know it in communion with the Holy Spirit. What is the central basis for their beliefs and the nourishment that satisfied their interior longing? Again, it was their unique desire to become one in the Truth; for God was telling them both, along with all the Saints, that it is borne only through the insuperable power of human Love. This is the same Almighty Father speaking to us now through the Wisdom of the Holy Paraclete who gave such dignity and foresight to the faith of His followers, many among them who marched wilfully to their deaths at the hands of His outraged enemies; some of whom were eviscerated, incinerated, beheaded, and tossed like rubbish into their cinder bins. Indeed, God knew from the outset that their oblation, not unlike ours today, would be required to be fed from the very depths of His Grace; and therefore, we are granted the Seven Holy Sacraments of the Roman Catholic Church. We become the likeness of the Victim on the Cross by participating in His Holy Sacrifice. The offensive lesions that human life leaves on our souls require a dressing and healing that only the Almighty King for whom we endure them could possibly provide.

While He always bears our griefs and carries our sorrows, we are to become His courageously principled Body of Mystical Truth in the modern-day world, confronting with valor the triple-headed beast of exhaustion, hatred, and despair as a portion of our suffering in emulating His agonizing Passion and Death. Jesus knew this before the beginning of the ages commenced; and His persevering Spirit sustains our conformity in Him through Christianity on the Earth today. Humanity has been given a collection of outward signs of His inward Grace; something powerfully binding and possessing of the sacred character and mysterious significance of God's loyalty to the very people He has dispatched His Son to Redeem; and they, thereafter, have become the new law.

The Sacraments of the Church

Baptism
Confirmation
Confession
The Holy Eucharist
Anointing of the Sick
The Holy Orders
Holy Matrimony

According to Saint Thomas Aquinas, the Holy Sacraments imbue all the stages of our mortal life by transferring our temporal existence into the supernatural process of God's perpetual Eternity, giving new birth to our spirits, rescuing us from the vile pestilence of sin, allowing our interior pain to convalesce, and providing a new direction and foundation to those persons who have entered the apostolic discipleship of the faithful elect. While there are Seven Sacraments as listed above that are received as our participation in the Life of Christ, I believe it to be wholly imperative for us to remember, as the Catholic Church has been so inclined to profess, that the Most Blessed among them is the Holy Eucharist. Why? Because the Sacred Host is the *physical* presence of Jesus Christ in the material world; and that we are quite capable of seeing Him with our very own eyes of faith, savoring His Sacred Flesh on the surface of our tongue, sheathing His Holy Spirit within the confines of the heart and, indeed, implanting His Resurrection in the fallows of our soul, fully acknowledging His residence there as being humanity-Divine to its fullest extent. This is our capacity and potential for refining the coarseness of our inequities and returning to the Almighty Father someday having already been stately clad in sartorial eminence for such an auspicious occasion. The Most Blessed Sacrament is the Living Body, Blood, Soul, and Divinity of Jesus' Crucified Flesh which is brought to Earth during the Eucharistic Celebration of the Holy Sacrifice of the Mass. Those who protest against this fact are in for the shock of their lives when they fully comprehend the immeasurable degree by which our Father God has loved us. Perhaps it would be appropriate to remind them of *The Eucharistic Miracle at Lanciano Italy*, where there lived a Basilian Monk around the year A.D. 700. According to the stated record of events, *"...he could not bring himself to believe that at the words of consecration uttered by him over bread and wine, their substances became the Body and Blood of Jesus Christ. But, being a devout priest, he continued to celebrate the Sacrament according to the teaching of the Church and begged God to remove the doubt from him. One day, as he was offering the Holy Sacrifice, following the words of consecration, the bread literally changed into (Jesus') Flesh and the wine into (His) Blood. At first, he was overwhelmed by what he saw. Then, regaining his composure, he called the faithful present to come to the Altar to see what the Lord had caused to happen."* (Association of Marian Helpers, Congregation of Marians, Stockbridge, Massachusetts, 1986).

The elements were not consumed from that Holy Mass, but were placed into an ivory container where they were carefully sheltered for nearly a thousand more years. The Blood eventually coagulated into five articulate globules. In 1713, they were enshrined in a majestic silver monstrance in which they have been preserved at the Church of St. Francis in Lanciano. In November 1970, at the urging of the Holy See, a team of forensic doctors that was chaired by Dr. Odoardo Linoli, a regarded professor of Anatomy and Pathological Histology, Chemistry, and Microscopy, was convened to discover their discernable nature. The committee had prepared a report of findings by March 1971 which concluded that both the Flesh and Blood belonged to the human species, that the Flesh consisted of myocardium muscular tissue of the heart, that the Flesh and the Blood had the same type AB; there were proteins in the Blood with the same percentile-proportions that are found in the composition of fresh normal human blood; the Blood contained chlorides, phosphorous, magnesium, potassium, sodium, and calcium—all consistent with the properties of human beings, and that the preservation of the Flesh and Blood which had been left in their original state for 1,200 years without the application of any preservatives and after exposure to the influences of atmospheric and biological agents remained an inexplicable miracle. When Pope John Paul II was Cardinal of Cracow, Poland, he visited the site of *The Eucharistic Miracle* at Lanciano, Italy on November 3, 1974. He expressed his devotion to the Shrine by signing the guest-book with the following inscription, "Make us always to believe more in you, to have hope in you, and to love you," reciting the Eucharistic Hymn of St. Thomas. To what might humanity attribute this supernatural gift from God's Sacred Altar in Heaven? That His desire is for us to recognize the significance of the Most Blessed Sacrament as our own thanksgiving for the Sacrifice of Our Lord on the Cross in expiation for our sins and transgressions. The Catholic Church recalls Jesus' words as they appear in the Holy Gospel, *"... While they were eating, Jesus took bread, said the blessing, broke it, and giving it to His disciples said, 'Take and eat; this is My Body.' Then, He took the Cup, gave thanks, and gave it to them saying, 'Drink from it, all of you; for this is My Blood of the Covenant, which will be shed on behalf of many for the forgiveness of sins.'"* (Matthew 26:26, cf. Mark 14:22-24, Luke 22:19-20, and 1 Corinthians 11:24).

Herein this Scriptural passage, we discover the factual knowledge that our Divine Lord instituted the Sacrament of the Holy Eucharist during the Last Supper in the Upper Room on the Maundy-evening before He died on the Cross the following day. Forever after, we are proud to proclaim that His Dying has destroyed our death, and His Rising from the Sepulcher has restored our life. This is how the Last Supper and Our Lord's Crucifixion are miraculously superimposed upon the Holy Altar of Sacrifice during the Eucharistic Liturgy as Good Friday is broadly spread over Creation beyond the timely parameters of the sorrowful hours in which it transpired. And, by worthily participating in it, we become the earthen vessels who carry the precision of His distinct holiness into the present day, just as armaments and provisions are borne from one rampart to the next. This is our time to fan the blazing steeples of our fiery compliance with God's Divine Love by transferring His single Torch of Truth through the multiple generations, passing it forward in history to keep our flame of faithfulness burning long after our teachers and mentors have gone to their graves. When we partake of Holy Communion, we embark upon a vast and heralded journey over the pristine acreage of the previously unexplored divinity of our mortal souls. The Most Blessed Sacrament is our reunion with perfection that enlivens the statuary arts of our inner-spirits and provides fluidity to our thoughts of eternal glee. While we cannot yet see these things as they are ongoing, the human soul is sanctified and made otherwise entirely incorruptible when we consume the Sacrificed Body of Christ. No form of elation is barred from participating in the continuous exaltation of our resurrection in this timeless march toward Life Everlasting as every grand, seamless, and knighted excellence is summoned from the higher Dominion of Paradise to reside within us here on the Earth. The very moment the Sacred Host commingles with our spiritually-hungry palate, the entire institution of Christianity, itself, is fed by way of our revised and universal holiness; rendering us to be God's newborn recruits and sworn commissioners for a destiny of unequivocal Light. The Most Blessed Sacrament is His Divine shelter in its finest hour; altogether revealing, inseparable, replenishing, reparative, offertorial, and inclusive. When it seems like we have waited for a lifetime to engage a reunion with the sacred-unknown, receiving the Holy Eucharist is our transfer into the glorified preeminence of Dietetical Love while we still reside in human flesh. God begins to communicate with us in ways that we could never before comprehend; and our relationship with the entire of humanity finally makes sense because a thousand ages in the sight of Jesus Christ become just as instrumental in our world today. There are no illusions as to *who* we are, where we are stationed between time and Eternity, or what would be the worth of looking back at all. The extremely complex and multifaceted aspects of our intellectual psyche begin to diminish in importance as we are drawn closer to the ecclesiastical presence of the future-world and away from our enamored infatuation with cumulative statistics. And, the bombardment and backlashing by which we conduct the affairs of life these days before the facade of ordinary time are excised in the process of our matriculation into the essential Providence of excelling Love because; through the Body, Blood, Soul, and Divinity of Christ, we are unleashed from the mundane, unchained from the chagrined, liberated from the casual, and transported beyond the defiance of the Earth and skies into the bosom of our rationally emotive God.

The Holy Sacrifice of the Mass helps us see our childhood years again from the other side of the galaxy and makes our sharpened intuition so refined that we can envision in our hearts the first drop of water that ever caused a stream to form, and the last to make it overflow. Our capacity to transcend the normal into the spiritually Divine causes our piousness to become an ancillary agent in the discernment of the physical globe because the Truth of God's Love is finally one and openly apparent to us. Hereafter, regional terrains are no longer defined by scopes, compasses, and transits because their meaning has been transformed in our consciousness to one of creative participation instead of appearing to be a surveyed deposit of organic plats.

We discover that the wind and breezes can be measured in cubic feet of height, width, and length; as well as direction and velocity. All of this distilled awareness of Heaven and Earth becomes ours during our participation in the Holy Sacrifice of the Mass. Our future was previously held in jeopardy because our souls were indicted for our sinfulness and we were sentenced to capital death; but the Most Blessed Sacrament is God's confirmation that the charges against us have been dismissed without prejudice and we are free to walk in innocence again. Our absolution is convened *within* us now because Jesus is alive at the center of our being; and His Father in Paradise would never forsake the Slain Christ Child in whom humanity has gained Eternal Redemption. The world has garnered a transparent perception of the entire of Creation through the celebration of the beatific Masses over which we have been poring for twenty centuries now. We have found that our previous arguments, stockpiled evidence, and inventoried opposition against the sublime existence of Paradise have been tainted by our personal weaknesses, lacking of accurate vision, and our inordinate desires to alter the meaning of the Truth. If there was only some way that we could coax our eyes into opening almost instantaneously by standards of moments instead of decades, we would be better able to secure the reasoning behind the fabricated vistas, visors, and novas of our social interaction which often take centuries to unfold and retroactively dissolve in the normal life-span of human events. Such an emphatic capturing of our spiritual conscience occurs when we receive the Eucharistic Host during Holy Mass and drink from the Chalice of Our Lord's Crimson Blood. As for me and the present day, I do not profess to be a writer who is capable of rendering captivating novels and holistic anthologies that are fodder for the *New York Times* Best Sellers List or paradigms of logistical thinking; nor am I even slightly capable of discovering the secrets of the inexplicable mysteries of the universe. However, I do know the power of the Holy Spirit when God becomes lodged inside a newly-converted heart belonging to a confirmed Catholic who worthily receives the Most Blessed of all the Sacraments. For those who do not yet know it, its grace is the source and cohesion of all human paranormal Wisdom, the healing for any type of infirmity, and the sound basis for all Christian faith.

For the record, I did not graduate from some elitist parochial high school or receive a Degree in Law or Divinity from an Ivy League college; neither have I learned about the existence of God by traveling to see the most holy relics or the greatest monuments on the Earth to discover His presence there. I have come to know His overpowering Love through the holiness of

His humble priests in lowly places: in the rural countryside, greeting them on the walkways between the barber shop and the grocery store, and watching them pour-out their lives with great suffering in small parishes and stately cathedrals in the backwoods of the USA. It is by virtue of their example that I acknowledge and understand that the strength of the pure-hearted power of improvisation which we gain from receiving the Most Blessed Sacrament is fruitfully poised in our response to the Holy Paraclete; while in this, and only in this, have our better venues been accorded for our expression of every beautiful rendition of poetry and prose in print and atop our closet shelves, our artistic masterpieces and musical scores, and all the biblical paraphrases of Christian religiosity that ever passed through the lips of a penitent sinner or from the pen of our greatest liturgical homilists. The intercession of the Holy Spirit is Heaven's prefigured dissolution of the language barriers between foreign nations and the obsolescence of every burial vault and skyward cenotaph; as all Creation has become singularly one and enveloped by the guardianship of legitimate perfection, saturated by the Blood of the Cross, embraced by The Divine Mercy, and repatriated into the ornate meadows and gateway thoroughfares of the New Jerusalem by Our Lord's sorrowful Crucifixion. Now and hereafter, there is no room for consternation anymore because the value and facility of interpersonal debate and private conjecture have expired, are gone, and will be forever passed. Through the Holy Eucharist that our priests have laid on the Altar of Sacrifice, we have learned to see the universe with much more patience than we ever did before, and we realize that humankind more often than not approaches us with courtesy than outright malevolence and disdain. Now, the designs of America can actually become a function of good judgment over expediency again; true enlightenment *can* exist in the darkness of our lost crevices; our challenges will always be overcome by our resolve; and the making of our modern ingenuity is only one more suppliance away. This is the peace and Truth to which we are called as a fruit of our union with Jesus Christ in His Eucharistic Host; to live in valor instead of fear; to judge *not* lest we be judged, and to become new stewards of the Earth to replace the many who are now passing into their Eternal reward. And, speaking of Nature, it has always amazed me how certain birds in the wild move their bodies with erratic flinches instead of imitating the smooth and silk-like motion of swans floating on a lake. Should we not also adhere to this contrast and make our lives stroll more gracefully across the vastness of the ages than the climactic hitches that our biographers and historians will wish to record in our posthumous days? We lurch around like wrens and crows sometimes, pecking at the surface of life as though we are too afraid of becoming involved in transforming the globe into the likeness of Heaven. We have a distance to travel before our peace can be described as an imitation of the dance of the soaring sea gulls overhead or the flight-path of the swallowtail butterflies.

Once we become children of the Light, the brief and casual glances we often proffer to Jesus Christ will become the absolute entrainment of our spiritual focus upon His priceless ingenuity; our embers of hope will be changed into reality afire; the equestrian foals in our imagination will grow into stampeding herds of accomplished deeds; and the best of what we can say about the Divine intervention of the Paradise we have regained will pale the ceremonial high-flying oratories of newly-crowned empresses and the patriotic speeches of monarchial queens as the Holy Spirit christens the Earth with peace, Love, and justice once again. The age of the ancient petrification of humankind's battle-worn spirits and vengeful hearts has passed-away with the Old World and, whether we like it or not, Creation has made it to within an inch of reaching the Morning Dawn, if only we can endure the wait a little longer while God's faithful Christians continue to conquer the night. All the travelers, sailors, hitchhikers, and vagabonds are at the brink of making it to their destination in what they have heretofore not even known they were seeking; and the Holy Eucharist is the hallmark and final milestone in the journey of them all toward their rite of passage into another life. There is no question or whit of doubt that we have suddenly donned a strange resourcefulness we never knew before; and all this has been slowly unveiling for the past 2,000 years by the invocation, prayerfulness, obedience, and servitude of our holy priests who have been so kind as to enter the religious life and bring the sacramental Kingdom of God to the Earth. If only we could gain some sense of the incalculable pondering that Our Divine Lord must be doing just beyond the reach of the stars to thank them in return, we would be overwhelmingly startled by His heartfelt gratitude that is surely beyond anything imaginable, conventional, nuclear, or even metaphysical we ever thought could previously exist. In the same stroke of genius, God does not require us to search the distant parlours of Creation to discover His Scriptural authority for the capacity of His priests to consecrate the gifts of Bread and Wine into His Sacred Body and Blood. The St. Joseph's Bible is cited as the origin of this powerful manifestation toward the basis and foundation of our faith in the miracle of the Eucharist. The entire Catechism of the Catholic Church has bloomed from the Word of God, as the beginning of all the Sacraments is soundly positioned there. As for the Holy Eucharist, itself, there are seven sections therein which describe the Sacrificed Body and

Blood of Jesus as our completion into Christian initiation. While I assuredly wish everyone would procure the Catechism and read about this all-important grace from Heaven, I will cite some excerpts from it here to provide a cursory purview of its content, taken from Part Two, Section Two, Article 3.

I. The Eucharist - Source and Summit of Ecclesial Life

> 1325   *"The Eucharist is the efficacious sign and sublime cause of that communion in the divine life and that unity of the People of God by which the Church is kept in being. It is the culmination both of God's action sanctifying the world in Christ and of the worship men offer to Christ and through Him to the Father in the Holy Spirit."*

II. What is this Sacrament called?

> 1329   *"The Lord's Supper, because of its connection with the supper which the Lord took with His disciples on the eve of His Passion, and because it anticipates the wedding feast of the Lamb in the heavenly Jerusalem."* (1 Corinthians 11:20, cf. Revelations 19:9).

> 1330   *"...the Memorial of the Lord's Passion and Resurrection. The Holy Sacrifice, because it makes present the one Sacrifice of Christ the Savior and includes the Church's offering. The terms 'Holy Sacrifice of the Mass, Sacrifice of Praise, Spiritual Sacrifice, Pure and Holy Sacrifice,' are also used since it completes and surpasses all the sacrifices of the Old Covenant. The Holy and Divine Liturgy because the Church's whole Liturgy finds its center and most intense expression in the celebration of this Sacrament; in the same sense, we also call its celebration the Sacred Mysteries."* (Hebrews 13:15, cf. 1 Peter 2:5, Psalm 116:13,17; and Malachi 1:11).

III. The Eucharist in the Economy of Salvation

> 1337   *"The Lord, having loved those who were His own, loved them to the end. Knowing that the hour had come to leave this world and return to the Father, in the course of a meal, He washed*

their feet and gave them the commandment of Love. In order to leave them a pledge of this Love, in order never to depart from His own and to make them sharers in His Passover, He instituted the Eucharist as the memorial of His death and Resurrection, and commanded His apostles to celebrate it until His return, 'thereby He constituted them priests of the New Testament.'" (Council of Trent, 1562: DS 1740).

IV. The Liturgical Celebration of the Eucharist

1346   *"The Liturgy of the Eucharist unfolds according to a fundamental structure which has been preserved throughout the centuries, down to our day. It displays two great parts that form a fundamental unity; (i) the gathering, the Liturgy of the Word, readings, homily, and general intercessions; (ii) the Liturgy of the Eucharist, with the presenting of the bread and wine, the consecratory thanksgiving, and communion. The Liturgy of the Word and Liturgy of the Eucharist form 'one single act of worship,' the Eucharistic table set for us is the table both of the Word of God and of the Body of the Lord."*

V. The Sacramental Sacrifice: Thanksgiving, Memorial, Presence

1357   *"We carry-out this command of the Lord by celebrating the memorial of His Sacrifice. In doing so, we offer to the Father what He has, Himself, given us: the gifts of His Creation, bread and wine which, by the power of the Holy Spirit and by the words of Christ, have become the Body and Blood of Christ. Christ is thus really and mysteriously made present."*

1358   *"We must consider the Eucharist as: (i) thanksgiving and praise to the Father, (ii) the sacrificial memorial of Christ and His Body, and (iii) the presence of Christ by the power of His Word and of His Spirit."*

VI. The Paschal Banquet

1382   *"The Mass is at the same time, and also inseparably, the sacrificial memorial in which the Sacrifice of the Cross is perpetuated and the sacred banquet of Communion with the*

Lord's Body and Blood. The celebration of the Eucharistic Sacrifice is wholly directed toward the intimate union of the faithful with Christ through Communion. To receive Holy Communion is to receive Christ, Himself, who has offered Himself for us."

1393 *"Communion separates us from sin. The Body of Christ we receive in Holy Communion is 'given up for us,' and the Blood we drink 'shed for the many for the forgiveness of sins.' For this reason, the Eucharist cannot unite us to Christ without at the same time cleansing us from past sins and preserving us from future sins (ff.)"*

1396 *"The unity of the Mystical Body: the Eucharist makes the Church. Those who receive the Eucharist are united more closely to Christ. Through it, Christ unites them to all the faithful in one body—the Church. Communion renews, strengthens, and deepens this incorporation into the Church, already achieved by Baptism. In Baptism, we have been called to form but one body. The Eucharist fulfills this call: '...the cup of blessing which we bless, is it not a participation in the Blood of Christ? The Bread which we break, is it not a participation in the Body of Christ? Because there is one Bread, we who are many are one body, for we all partake of the one Bread."* (1 Corinthians 12:13, 10:16-17).

VII. The Eucharist - " Pledge of the Glory to Come"

1404 *"The Church knows that the Lord comes even now in His Eucharist and that He is here in our midst. However, His presence is veiled. Therefore, we celebrate the Eucharist '...awaiting the blessed hope and the coming of our Savior, Jesus Christ,' asking '...to share in your Glory when every tear will be wiped away. On that day, we shall see you, our God, as you are! We shall become like you and praise you forever through Christ our Lord."* (EP III 116: Prayer for the Dead.)

1405   *"There is no surer pledge or clearer sign of this great hope in the new heavens and new earth '...in which righteousness dwells,' than the Eucharist. Every time this sacred mystery is celebrated, '...the work of our Redemption is carried-on,' and we '...break the one Bread that provides the medicine of immortality, the antidote for death, and the food that makes us live forever in Jesus Christ.'"* (2 Peter 3:13, and Saint Ignatius of Antioch).

By proper facility, it is quite obvious that the Holy Eucharist is the central and Most Blessed of the Sacraments of the Church, from which all the rest evolve. Do we not celebrate The Lord's Supper in conjunction with the Baptism of our children, the weddings of our brides and grooms, the ordination of our new deacons and priests, and during the sacred Rite of Christian Burial? Again, for the sake of brevity and the relative nature of the discussion at hand, I would beseech each and every one alive who is hoping to gain Eternal Salvation in the Blood of Jesus someday to secure a copy of the Catechism and become absorbed in and consumed by the profound description of the other Sacraments which are listed there. I have reserved the entire next Chapter for the expressed purpose of expounding upon the Rite of Reconciliation because I know from firsthand experience the power which is inherent therein. As for the Sacraments of Baptism, Confirmation (Chrismation), the Holy Orders, the Sacrament of Matrimony, and Anointing of the Sick (cf. Extreme Unction), I would be sorely remiss if I did not include an abbreviated recollection of them here. It is stated concisely in the Catechism that the Sacraments of Baptism, Confirmation, and the Eucharist lay-out the foundations of every Christian life. Baptism provides our freedom from the labors of our inherited sins and bathes us clean of the stain which was heaped upon us by the original sin of Adam and Eve in the Garden of Eden. The term "baptize" signifies that our soul is united in the waters of this Sacrament to symbolize our own burial into the death of Christ; whereupon He raises us up in newness by virtue of the power of His Paschal Resurrection. *"...so, whoever is in Christ is a new creation: the old things have passed-away; behold, new things have come. And, all this is from God, who has reconciled us to Himself through Christ and given us the ministry of reconciliation, namely God was reconciling the world to Himself in Christ, not counting their trespasses against them and entrusting to us the message of reconciliation. So, we are ambassadors for Christ, as if God were appealing through us. We implore you on behalf of Christ, be reconciled to God."* (2

Corinthians 5:17-20, cf. Galatians 6:15, Romans 6:34, and Colossians 2:12). The Catechism states that our Baptism is also referred to as *"...the washing of regeneration and renewal by the Holy Spirit,"* for it manifests our birthing in water and the Spirit, without which, no soul is allowed entrance into Heaven. (Part Two, Section Two, Article 1, 1215). Perhaps the most prescient summation of Baptism has been left to us through the writings of Saint Gregory of Nazianzus, who is quoted in the Catechism of the Catholic Church for his enlightened perception of the faith-filled miracle of its institution. *"...Baptism is God's most beautiful and magnificent gift... We call it gift, grace, anointing, enlightenment, garment of immortality, bath of rebirth, seal, and most precious gift. It is called 'gift' because it is conferred on those who bring nothing of their own; 'grace' since it is given even to the guilty; 'Baptism' because sin is buried in the water; 'anointing' for it is both as priestly and royal as are those who are anointed; 'enlightenment' because it radiates light; 'clothing' since it veils our shame; 'bath' because it washes; and 'seal' as it is our guard and the sign of God's Lordship."* (*Oratio* 40, 3-4: PG 36, 361C). Ritual has it that most adult catechumens are baptized during the Solemn Easter Vigil celebration at the end of the Season of Lent. There are occasions, however, when infants are Baptized during the entire Liturgical Year.

The Sacrament of Confirmation occurs when the faithfully baptized are summoned under oath and before the witness of the Church to declare their Profession of Faith publicly, wilfully, and dutifully. This Sacrament is also known as "Chrismation" because an anointing Oil of Chrism is spread in the Sign of the Cross upon the forehead of the one being confirmed to mark his soul with the seal of the Holy Spirit. Referencing the Catechism once again, *"...the pre-baptismal Anointing with the oil of catechumens signifies cleansing and strengthening; the Anointing of the Sick expresses healing and comfort. The post-baptismal anointing with sacred Chrism in Confirmation and Ordination is the sign of consecration. By Confirmation, Christians, that is those who are anointed, share more completely in the mission of Jesus Christ and the fullness of the Holy Spirit with which He is filled, so that their lives may give-off the aroma of Christ."* (Part Two, Section Two, Article 2, 1294; cf. 2 Corinthians 2:15). Similar oils are used to anoint those who are ordained into the religious life and others who are suffering illness and sickness. According to the Council of Trent (1551: DS 1697), only priests, bishops, and presbyters are allowed to administer The Sacrament of the Anointing of the Sick. (Catechism, Article 5, 1516). It is given to those who are feeling indisposed by reason of physical, spiritual, or emotional infirmity; as well as for the homebound and people who are suffering from grave illness or are otherwise in danger of impending death. In addition to this, the Church invites those who are at the verge of dying to receive the Holy Eucharist as a *viaticum*, i.e.,*"...Communion in the Body and Blood of Christ, received at this moment of 'passing over' to the Father, has a particular significance and importance. It is the seed of Eternal Life and the power of Resurrection, according to the words of the Lord: '...he who eats My Flesh and drinks My Blood has Eternal Life, and I will raise him up at the last day.' The Sacrament of Christ once dead and now Risen, the Eucharist is here the Sacrament of passing-over from death to Life, from this world to the Father."* (Catechism, Part Two, Chapter Two, Article 5, 1524; cf. John 6:54; John 13:1). The Roman Catholic Church recommends that the Sacraments of Baptism, Confirmation, and the Eucharist define the entirety of Christian initiation, while the Rite of Confession as described in Chapter VII of this book, Anointing of the Sick, and Eucharistic Communion confer the end of a Christian life, *"...the Sacraments that prepare for our heavenly homeland; the Sacraments that complete the earthly pilgrimage."* (Article 5, 1525). We note with emphasis that the Holy Eucharist is our spiritual food at the beginning, during, and at the conclusion of our mortal existence here on Earth. And, with the providence of the Holy Orders and Matrimony clearly explicated in the Roman Catechism, the Sacraments of Salvation are firmly in place and made known by the Church as their power is dispensed from the Throne of the Father in Heaven. Each of them is founded upon the Holy Gospel and further beatified by the works of the Communion of Saints. The Divine intercession of the Paraclete of the Triune Deity is the grace-filled mediator through which each of them is authenticated by God. We are not without credible representation beyond the parameters of the mortal world because, just as the Sacraments themselves are ordained in Heaven, our relationship with Jesus Christ is augmented, emboldened, and enhanced as we comply in faith with their stated decrees. The Sacraments are more than God's vicarious experiencing of our own personal agonies or the sublime empathy that any other father would hold for his children. We are oftentimes made into scapegoats in the wiles of a tawdry exile of grief and shambles because of the evil of Satanic works; and Jesus Christ knows that it is only through His intervention that we can walk the narrow path toward the Paradisial Gate of Eternal Sanctification. He dispenses the Sacraments to us, *and us to the Sacraments,* to enhance our relationship not only with the Kingdom of God, but between ourselves as hapless sinners. Without Holy Matrimony, for example, would there be a promise of inner-sanctity in everything we do and say with the mother or father of our infant children? God is looking for commitment from us; and the Sacraments of human Salvation define the courses of action which keep us in alignment with the virtues of Immortal Love.   He not only presides over our religious ceremonies as they are described in the Holy Gospel, His Spirit of Divine perfection lives inside our hearts to help us uphold our pledge and promise to be reconciled to one another in all we do for Christ through the evocative proficiency of His Grace.

Chapter VII
The Penitential Rite of Confession

"The reason why we are not better than we are is that we do not 'will' to be better: the sinner and the Saint are set apart only by a series of tiny decisions within our hearts. Opposites are never so close as in the realm of the spirit: an abyss divides the poor from the rich, and one may cross it only with the help of external circumstances and good fortune. The dividing line between ignorance and learning is also deep and wide: both leisure to study and a gifted mind would be required to turn an ignoramus into a learned man. But, the passage from sin to virtue, from mediocrity to sanctity requires no 'luck,' no help from outer circumstances. It can be achieved by an efficacious act of our own wills in cooperation with God's Grace."

His Excellency, Bishop Fulton Sheen, D.D.
From *The Way to Happiness*
Part X, Chapter 57, 1949

The Sacrament of Confession deserves and requires its own chapter in the annals of human history because it is at the veritable center of our spiritual conversion in accepting Christianity and the Sacred Blood of the Crucifixion of Jesus Christ on the Cross as atonement for our sins. It is also called the Sacrament of Penance, Forgiveness, and Reconciliation. The First Chapter of St. Mark's Gospel states that this is the time of fulfillment for all the Earth; and we are therefore called to our repentance because the Kingdom of God is at hand. Indeed, the entire foundation of our expression of self-mortification is to realize that we have sinned. In the parable of the Prodigal Son in Chapter 15 in the Holy Gospel according to St. Luke, the son acclaims that he will return to his father and confess that he has sinned against both Heaven and him. Hence, the Rite of Reconciliation is one of the Seven Holy Sacraments of the Roman Catholic Church. At least once in the life of every person whose soul is bound for Paradise, there must be a realization and an examination of conscience wherein he acknowledges his culpability as a party in the body of humankind who has been disloyal to the statutes and ordinances of God, has betrayed the Archangels, and violated the Saints who reside beyond the scope of our immediate vision. Why? Because we are all still constrained by the infamy and ill-gotten modernism of the everyday world from seeing the Eternal Light of Truth and Love with the perfection we need to deploy our Christian faith effectively. The wondering mind and withering heart of someone who is steeped in sin can never lead his spirit back to happiness because there is nothing even slightly pure or divine in espousing, avowing, or participating in any transgression that keeps our soul separated from the excellence of the endless sanctity of Jesus Christ. Our mortal lives are a sojourn through a dark and tempestuous gauntlet of fear and doubt; but we are not left alone to wallow in the mire of our corruption because the power of the Cross has become our internal deliverance to an amended course of external achievement. We often misunderstand what it means to live in the absence of war because the world has grown so accustomed to waging it as a misguided means of effecting change. I am not calling for the same kind of "peace" by which we were confronted in the late-1960s when our teen-age children waved their medius and index fingers in front of our faces in the sign of a "V" and smiled with a casual blank stare. In the reasoning of (the late) Bishop Fulton Sheen, whatever we do to alter the face of the globe so as to make it a reflection of Heaven must begin with the actual *Spirit* of Peace, who is the Son of God, alive and elucidated from the very core and aspect of our mortal being.

If we ever gave Jesus Christ the fundamental opportunity to reach our interior consciences by casting-away the physical distractions that keep us so at odds with His Divine overtures, our battles and skirmishes over material wealth and landownership would suddenly disappear, rendering humankind to be standing innocently unclad before the crest, summits, and peaks of galvanized Love, Justice, and Truth. While there are certainly giants among us who undoubtedly know Him best; this does not infer that He realizes the fate of the rest of us any less. And, this is why we are called to dispel the day of every superfluous detail and intricacy that makes men slaves to the computer modem and idle spectators beside a larger field-line of measurable human achievement. If we cared as much about fasting and prayer for our spiritual deficiencies with as much emphasis as some people anticipate their next tummy-tuck, we might be able to sublimate our carnal cravings in favor of the higher beatitudes of volitional self-denial and pious reparation. These are among the chief properties upon which we should be meditating when we think about what our standing might be beyond the Gate of Paradise on any given day. For now, however, our progress seems to be vised between slothfulness and indifference because of our outright refusal to admonish one another to do any better toward the conversion of humanity-entire. For this, we are all a lesser people and a mosaic collage of closed societies that are still willing to live in segregation between the seas; away from global unity, in defiance of the Commandments of God, and certainly shy of the resolve required to even engage the discussion. These are the attributes of our failures in undertaking the task of ushering the Kingdom of God into our contemporary world. *If we are all to blame, then each of us must surely be equally as guilty as individual citizens.* And, by every apportioned deduction, the cure and amendment must begin at the center of our hearts. Every seed beneath the ground must grow of its own accord, neither invoking the strength nor approximating the posture of any of its kind in its midst. And, we are the subterranean beginnings of the new life of goodness for Christ around the globe. If we start from within, we can make a larger difference without. This is the profession to which we are called; the humility of faith by which we will succeed in knowing ourselves with clearer identity. In the final analysis, we live as one among many, and we must beseech God to penetrate each of us individually to make us free from prejudice, take us to the heights of His glorified presence, and render us willing to confess what we know to be true about ourselves today and the record of our past. Why is this larger discussion about humanity relative to the Sacrament of Penance? Because the interrogation of the self results in the improvement of our interpersonal conduct, the enhancement of our Christian values, and the mending of our lives. Once we have received the Rite of Reconciliation, we are a renewed Creation under the auspices of the ecclesia; and we are fully expected to refrain from repeating our sins once our confession has been heard and absolution dispensed. God might look rather poorly upon someone who barely examines his conscience, reenters this Sacrament, and is forced to say *ibid* because he has repeated the same course of error again. It is not that He declines to bestow pardon upon our soul "seventy-times-seven" times, but the Sacrament of Penance is not our license to commit further wanton infringement with the expectation that we are thereafter free to yield to the identical circumstances which first led to our spiritual and corporal offenses.

All this having been said, would it be too presumptuous for us to assume that all the waves crashing against the oceanic shores of the Earth are the tears of our Almighty Father having overflowed from Heaven onto the wetlands below because some of us are still lacking in faith and fear of His Justice in the wake of our earlier fall from grace? If we are truly going to be converted to the designs of His Plan for Salvation, do we not reckon that He knows that we are only little children whose thoughts and actions are neither as glib nor facile as the keen perspective that His miraculous spiritual Truth has given to those who have died in His grace? There is no doubt that our Creator is capable of forming His own equitable judgment about our moral qualities because of the pastoral guidance of His priests who teach us to be upright and who administer the Sacrament of Penance on His behalf. Let us be clear: it is God, Himself, who forgives sinners in the Rite of Confession once He sees a penitent who is filled with contrition, remorse, compunction, and regret. Again, the Roman Catechism:

> 1431   *"Interior repentance is a radical reorientation of our whole life, a return, a conversion to God with all our heart, an end of sin, a turning away from evil, with repugnance toward the evil actions we have committed. At the same time, it entails the desire and resolution to change one's life, with hope in God's Mercy and trust in the help of His grace. This conversion of heart is accompanied by a salutary pain and sadness which the Fathers called 'affliction of the spirit' and 'repentance of the heart.'"* (Part Two, Section Two Chapter Two, Article 4).

> 1468   *"The whole power of the Sacrament of Penance consists in restoring us to God's grace and joining us with Him in an intimate friendship. Reconciliation with God is thus the purpose and effect of this Sacrament. For those who receive the Sacrament of Penance with contrite heart and religious disposition, reconciliation 'is usually followed by peace and serenity of conscience with strong spiritual consolation.' Indeed, the Sacrament of Reconciliation with God brings about a true 'spiritual resurrection,' restoration of the dignity and blessings of the life of the children of God, of which the most precious is friendship with God."* (Chapter Two, Article 4, IX).

The panoramic touchstone, thesis, and entire premise of this book; and the reason for the factual recitation of the past ninety pages, is to echo and reconfirm that the Sacrament of Confession renders those who receive it from an ordained and duly recognized priest innocent of their sins; both public and private; not liable to prosecution for past wrongdoings under any circumstance or venue, and vindicated *to the degree of absolute* before the backdrop of all seen and unseen Creation. When Jesus Christ told the world that "...he who is without sin may cast the first stone," He was, beyond any doubt, referring equally to the matters of our modern-day as He was to those who were standing in His midst twenty-centuries ago. Why are our mothers so afraid that their children will stumble and fall on the path to maturity in America today? It is not that their progeny might be too weak to rise and begin anew, but that the rest of humanity will never forgive them for failing the first time; and the dark cloud of stain and regret will haunt them for the rest of their lives. Our Western culture is prowling for juicy headlines; the media, the government, and the courts have made it their main directive to hold ordinary citizens in contempt for not complying with their definition of "perfection." There are millionaires all across the United States who are forwarding their agendas of vengeance and vile hatred in newspapers and via the radio and television industries in which they have invested their stocks and expendable cash. Lawyers who have been chasing ambulances for generations are now the enticement of the judicial system because they are the vehicle through which Roman Catholic parishioners are being persuaded to turn against the Church that is administering the very Sacraments of their Eternal Salvation for the prospect of gaining the promise of a transient cache of earthly wealth. The secular world refuses to accept both the power and effect of the Sacrament of Confession; and this is one of the reasons why they do not even remotely appear as a blip on the radar screen beside those who are flying in stately grace on their way to Paradise. Although we oftentimes see human interest stories about certain religious events in many of our nation's publications or on evening satellite documentaries, let there be no mistake; the American media are an enemy of the Catholic Church! Most of their correspondents could not care less about how much damage their reporting is doing to the reputation of formal Christianity or whether they, themselves, will ever be held accountable before the Throne of God for casting that first stone. If the Catholic Church is under a period of purification or a purging within itself, both time and Eternity will reveal that it has had nothing whatsoever to do with the hate-monger antics of our news agencies, judicial system, or mental healthcare industries. The present and ongoing phenomenon of the so-called "priest scandal" is no more than a headlong leap toward opportunism in which the adversaries of the Church are engaged for their own corporate and private financial gain. While the media-henchmen of North America are fishing for news headlines, God is looking downward from His Seat of Dominion in Paradise and shaking His head from side-to-side; snickering because so many who profess to be faithful Christians have entered the fields of law enforcement and social justice and have chosen to continue to Crucify Jesus by defying His Sacred Commandments in their efforts to overtly persecute the weak, prosecute the accused, and extort tens-of-millions of dollars in assets from the coffers of His Roman Catholic Church; all in the name of some hollow secular "reparation."

Those of us who believe in the Sacraments to the ends of the Earth can imagine the last day of linear time in our mind's eye as it begins to unfold. Our Divine Lord will physically come back into the world, alright; but what a moment that will bring to those who did not inherit a fortune from their parents, who never earned it on their own, and were not given the talent of sleight-of-hand in winning the games of chance. What will His answer be when those who are enjoying the spoils of their wealth are asked where they got it, and their answer will be, *"...we sued your Church because we were violated by those you chose to represent you here on Earth."* With a look of cold disdain in His eyes, He will then turn toward them with the remembrance of the Sacrament of Confession in His thoughts by which He has already forgiven His priests and tell their accusers; *"...I have no idea what in Hades you are talking about!"* Never-mind that there are already countless people crawling out of the woodwork these days, claiming to have been sexually molested and abused two and three decades earlier. Most of them are normal, prosperous, productive, and heterosexual parents of quite functional families. Why are they coming forward? Because their case is oftentimes based upon *their* word against that of their supposed violators in an environment where the accused are assumed to be guilty-as-charged with no semblance of due process. We can imagine the telephone-lines being jammed all across the country as certain people have a strange and sudden "recollection"about what allegedly occurred to them in one of their dreams. Do we remember the recantation of the accuser of (the late) Joseph Cardinal Bernardin of the Archdiocese of Chicago before His Eminence's death in November 1996? And, oh yes, what are they saying over the telephone? *Get in line, the gravy train is here!* There is no difference in the hysteria that is ongoing against the institution of the Roman Catholic priesthood than the same paranoia that engulfed America when Senator Joseph McCarthy was running around the country claiming that the entire U.S. government was infiltrated by Communists. This time, however, the scampering rodents and free-loaders stand to become filthy rich because they are attacking an organized religion which would rather get it all behind it and resume the course of converting lost souls to Christianity. There are hundreds-of-millions of silent supporters of the 47,000 Catholic priests in America and the many thousands around the globe who are sitting quietly in the wings, waiting for the smokescreen to disappear; watching Satan and his mountebanks peddle their story about the supposed falsehood of Divine Love and laughing aloud about the ruckus they have caused to distract God's bishops, priests, deacons, ministers, and pilgrims from doing His faithful works here on Earth. The American media do not really want this story to disappear for fear that they might lose a sordid headline, so they continue to hunt, root, prey, and runabout like decapitated chickens in an effort to create some false illusion that it is a much larger catastrophe than it really is. Lawyers are trembling in their shoes that the issue might die too soon for them to reap untold fortunes for their briefcase stashes. And, Catholic-haters of all colors and stripes are holding their breath until near-unconsciousness that this opportunity will have enough legs to finally bring the 2,000-year-old Roman Catholic Church to its knees that Jesus Christ, Himself, stood high, elegant, and proud on the Feast of Pentecost, 50 days after He was raised by God from the dead. While the Church maintains that the effects of certain inner-feelings and passions diminish the voluntary character of our weaknesses, such as external pressures and pathological disorders; the secular world claims no such exculpating factors to our faith in God, reminding us that when we fail to satisfy the whims of society, we are thereafter supposed to be regarded as aliens in the throes of a world of revenge and punishment, and unfit to be seen outside a prison cell without a ball and chain. This is the fallacious conspiracy of retaliation, requital, and vindictiveness that Jesus Christ will toss like chaff and goat carcasses into the fires of Gehenna.

Even though we may choose to believe that our dreams are dying and the portraiture of our immortal heritage which used to live so gracefully at the center of our spirits is slowly fading away, we can still gain new hope that the Love of God will strengthen and sustain our priests; and that His eternal justice will uphold the consummate purity of those who have never yielded to temptations of the flesh; while our Lord has already fully restored the innocence of the rest. I waited until the seventh chapter of this book to waylay their enemies because I did not wish to appear to be some crank, crackpot theologian, or a coltish zealot. Associated Press reporter Richard Ostling, whose work has regularly appeared in newspapers around the country about the incidence of priestly sexual abuse, was sufficiently fair in citing how the Roman Catholic Church has been unduly impugned in this discussion. Over the wire in April 2002, he said, *"...Penn State historian Philip Jenkins argued in his 1996 book, 'Pedophiles and Priests, '...media exaggerate the extent of Catholic cases involving minors, while downplaying Protestant abuse...Jenkins, an Episcopalian, thinks a 1992 survey from the Chicago Archdiocese is more representative of the true picture in Catholicism. Among 2,252 priest serving over four decades, 39 priests (1.7 percent) apparently abused minors. Only one abuser could be termed a pedophile under the strict, clinical definition of the word—meaning the victim was prepubescent, '...nobody has good data, partly because Protestant groups are too numerous...Minneapolis psychologist Gary Schoener agreed. 'There are no real scientific data on Protestants,' Since, 1974, his Walk-in Counseling Center has been consulted on more than 2,000 cases of clergy sexual misconduct of all types, two-thirds of them with Protestants."* The key in defining the finished product of a Christian soul is how we are vested in the grace of God both on the inside and outwardly. Were it not for the constraints of time and space, I would happily spend another fifty years detailing the overall degradation that the media have wrought upon our American nation. However, I have better things to do than waste any more time looking behind and stoning the devil's dogs. I think it was Tennyson who wrote, *"...that which we are, we are. One equal temper of heroic hearts. Made weak by time and fate, but strong in will."* I would like to add to his reflections that we can also be defined by the goodness we do; to the vast advancement of charity and faith, the ending of poverty and disease; and the elimination of international strife—all these things are our invitation to combat the world's evil by invoking the sublimities of Light, conversion, and spiritual intonation.

Whatever we might afford those who are the least among us bears no greater benevolence than the interior pardoning we must give to anyone who has offended us. This, in itself, is our emulation of the Light. If we listen carefully enough to the Holy Spirit as the Love of God runs smoothly through our veins, He will render us the words of absolution to offer clearly and audibly to our offenders; given that our hearts are truly open to live-out the mandates of our faith. Will we remember what Christ is teaching us through the Sacrament of Penance; not only as we seek His forgiveness, ourselves, but to the inclusion of all other men? There is no question that we are more than capable of granting anyone the plenary vindication they need and forgetting about their offenses thereafter; reaching completely beyond the yester-years and retrieving the visible innocence with which we rolled that first snowball down the hill on our grade-school playground or skimmed stones across the surface of the backwoods creek until we were frightened-away by the grumbling of a bear. There is plentiful room on the Earth for everyone who walks the pathways of life; and time is far too short for us to make a mockery of human absolution or hold someone's faults before the backdrop of Creation and hit them with a spotlight just because we can. The noble art of conflict resolution can be deployed effectively only through our mutual forgiveness. Indeed, we have already seen the fruits that it can bear in places around the globe where it has been used to the effectuation of a secured and lasting peace. No nation in either global hemisphere has any better example of the necessity for social unity than the United States of America after having seen the awful events of the mid-19th century Civil War from 1861-1865. And, the same cohesion between modern Christians is no-less important for the integrity of our faith. It seems as though tomorrow may never come; at least for now anyway; but this gives us reason and necessity to touch one another in a more positive way today. Yes, it is true that we are oftentimes defined by what we do, but there has never been any doubt that we are also *refined* by how well we love. If God has whet our appetite for a truer meaning of life, He has sent us His precise image in Jesus Christ for whom we must hunger; He who is our standard for spiritual and physical durability, the atypical personage of a restructured human species, and the blueprint and ground plan for what the inside of the heart was always meant to be. He is the synergy between God and man in the Holy Sacraments of the Church, the Prefect of Creation-entire, and the predominant force of all that is to come in the supernature of Heaven's grand outlays. He has molded us to be more than conquerors of hatred and injustice in a world that is still crying-out for repair and a will to change; for we are His sergeants and mace-bearers with the future of Love in our hands during the arrival of the end-times of the Earth.

Since One, for Love, Died on a tree
And, in the stony Tomb was lain,
Behold, I show a mystery:
All sepulchers are sealed in vain!

-John Richard Moreland

Fleur-de-Lis

Weep on, Sad Lily.
The things that you see
will not always be;
for those who are strong
and fancy and free
are too fragile and busy
to openly see
that all they have now
is lesser than thee!   (ii)
Weep for them, Lily!
Weep for their blindness.
Weep for their souls
and offer your kindness.
Your delicate petals are
perfect in form
as the soft velvet skin
of a tiny newborn.
'Til man enters in
where Nature has been
and corrupts the beauty
that once lay therein.   (iii)
Weep for them, Lily!
As they have their day
to do things their way;
'Til God finally demands
they all enter His Hands.
They'll then know their time
was much better spent
perceiving your beauty
and breathing your scent.   (iv)
Be not your sorrow in vain, little Lily!
They'll see when they've died
how much you have cried.
Be it never denied
that you're superior to them,
if they reject their Salvation
and your blooming again!

Timothy Parsons-Heather
November 29, 1975

Chapter VIII
Where Charity and Love Prevail

"Patience and patience, we shall win at the last. We must be very suspicious of the deceptions of the element of time. It takes a good deal of time to eat or to sleep, or to earn a hundred dollars, and a very little time to entertain a hope and an insight which becomes the light of our life. We dress our garden, eat our dinners, discuss the household with our wives, and these things make no impression, are forgotten next week; but, in the solitude to which every man is always returning, he has a sanity and revelations which, in his passage into new worlds, he will carry with him. Never mind the ridicule, never mind the defeat; up again, old heart!—it seems to say,—there is victory yet for all justice; and the true romance which the world exists to realize will be the transformation of genius into practical power."

Ralph Waldo Emerson
From *Experience*
1844

Humanity must discover a new way to escape all the intricacies, peripheries, boundaries, premieres, and precepts that make us so desirous of abandoning the broadness of our spiritual well-being before it is too late to turn back from having strayed so far from God through our ideological pragmatism that we find ourselves beyond the point of no return. It would surprise no one to know that even the existentialist notions of Emerson, himself, as beautifully prophetic as they may seem to be, are usurped by the circumspection of God's biblical Truth. Our 21st century world, especially here in America, is in need of a correction of course to the redefining of our international meaning; knowing well in advance that we are required to scrutinize every distinction that makes us intelligible from other republics so as to conjoin as a single humanity under the Cross. While the Church is still in the process of commissioning a decision as to the authenticity of the Marian apparitions in Medjugorje, Bosnia-Herzegovina, it is still fitting to cite one of the Blessed Virgin Mary's messages to the six pilgrim children there in October 1981, *"...The West has made civilized progress, but without God, as if they were their own creators."* This is from the Mother of Jesus Christ, Herself; spoken so profoundly through the power and Wisdom of the Holy Spirit that tens-of-millions have gone to this tiny Croatian village to hear it for themselves. I have been there; I have learned the Truth about the errors of our ways; and it is quite obvious after having seen the simplicity in which Our Lady is asking us to live that the United States is light-years away from the holiness that we will eventually be required to espouse, or risk the loss of our collective souls in the wake of our defiance and disinterest. I have incorporated a discussion about the Virgin Mary in Chapter X of this book to ensure our understanding of Her role in the conversion and Salvation of humanity. While She is the Queen of Heaven, the obvious purpose of Her Divine intercession is to draw our attention to the needs of the mortal world and what we must do to overcome the burdens of our exile from the Garden of Eden. We are urged to remember that our priests and spiritual advisors are the "pleats" in the tapestry of human purification as we continue to be held in suspension on the surface of the physical Earth by the elevated holiness which resides beyond the Firmament overhead. As the Catholic Catechism has indicated quite appropriately, we need to formally advance our "radical reorientation" back to the Kingdom of God at the expense of reducing our continuing enticements of corporeal temptation and material wealth. In the process, the Catholic Church must also be protected from being heaved into the gristmill of the faults and haughty indiscretions of the secular world, i.e., the works of partisan political strategists, photogenic "talking heads," and power-hungry realists.

There is no doubt that the Angels and Saints take great umbrage in our ignoring their role in the purification and refinement of the world, as well; for it is their intercession before God which keeps the lofty hopes of our children from careening into the cinder-coned valleys of despair and hopelessness when they seem unable to communicate with us anymore. After all, they are the least among us who are capable of grappling with the crass social atmosphere in which they are pummeled almost everyday in our schools, on the street, and over the publicized airwaves. As the Blessed Mother has been proclaiming for generations now, we must ensure that they accompany us in receiving the Sacraments of the Church on a regular basis; partaking in a daily examen of their conscience to determine if their spirituality is being slowly stripped-away from them by the hypnotic effects of living in the secular world. They should be shielded from the unbridled malice and rankling resentment of Satan's evil works by inviting them to pray with us in Christian contemplation and protecting them from falling prey to those who are self-proclaimed sworn enemies of the Cross. It is imperative that we teach the next generation of Americans to refrain from being enslaved by polytheism, materialism, and addiction to contraband and matters of the flesh. What corporate America is trying to peddle to them as being personal amenities according to our luxurious Western way of life are seen by those who follow the Christian Gospel to the letter of the law as a debris-field of expendable distractions that prohibit us from being more serious about our relationship with God.   What do we suppose can be deduced from the difficulties that modern Christians in America are facing today? We have almost certainly become the irreverent antithesis of the goodness that our more modest predecessors exuded. There is no doubt that the "one size fits all" prospect of approaching the Truth is no longer relevant in our age because so many in our ranks are claiming to have been somehow victimized by others in their midst. This seems to be abating as we speak, however, because the entire premise of " survival of the fittest" is slowly being diminished by the overwhelming power of God to change the world through the awful catastrophes He is allowing to occur in various places around the globe. It does very little to be the most vicious beast in the jungle when the God who has created it allows it to be positioned inside the cross-hairs of a hunter's scope or tethered like a lion being eaten alive by vultures with his hind foot stuck in a trap. This should give us pause to wonder what will become of us if we continue to take our right to hold dominion over the Earth for granted by abusing the privilege of procuring only the share we need for ourselves and not remembering the importance of preserving the dignity of those who depend on us for their sustenance. This is among the many virtues we must impress upon the conscience of our youth today if we are ever to reverse the trend that has brought even the Mother of Jesus Christ to say that we are behaving as though we are our own gods. Our crafty stratagem of interpersonal competition will be of little consequence once we fully comprehend the big picture in which we are all seen contained inside the same belly of unresolved human insolence, being slowly digested by the acidic enzymes of dispute, debate, contention, jealousy, and unparalleled prejudice.

It would behoove us to remember the September 29, 1937 entry in Sister Faustina's *Divine Mercy Diary* wherein she stated that she desired to enhance her relationship "...with *my* God." Jesus Christ, indeed, wants us to seek Him today with these same possessive overtones. We must conclude after the passing of centuries of time, the expedition of reams of Pastorals and Encyclicals, the exhaustion of thousands of Holy Hours, and an Eternity of Divine Wisdom that God can best be found on the Earth by our peers in what we, ourselves, say and do to invite Him in. It is going to require more than a hefty dint of good intentions to turn this world around, but also a perpetual collection of pious ejaculations. Our exertion should be specifically, solely, and explicitly toward advancing the Kingdom of God on the Earth and to prepare our mortal souls for the possibility that we will sometimes fall short of our goals. Again, we are not unlike our children in this regard because adults can slide into the same snares as the little ones we are attempting to lead. The question at hand is whether we own the gumption to fight against those who might try to sell us a parcel of land alongside the frozen lakes of the Mojave Desert without our ever stopping to wonder about the credibility of their claims or the perplexing motivations by which we have been approached from the start. This is the extent to which our collective American conscience has deteriorated in assuming that our friends and associates cannot be influenced by the tricks of the devil; and, in order to combat it, we must reorient our concentration to the Truth of the Holy Gospel in great masses so as to counteract the fallacies that impact our senses everyday in nearly seismic proportions. There are only three hours that should matter to us anymore; the ones that Jesus Christ hung on the Cross on Mount Calvary and bled so copiously for the eradication of our sins from noon until three o'clock in the afternoon on Good Friday. He is the sustaining and invariable Truth to which we must all return; the same sanity and revelations that even Ralph Waldo Emerson carried with him when he left this world and entered the next. Christ did not change colors like a chameleon to protect Himself from prosecution and torture during His trial before Pontius Pilate; nor did He attempt to amend the Truth to spare Himself from certain death. That is why we can remain constantly pure inside the safeguard of His Love as have God's living Saints in every century of the history of the Earth. His Passion and Crucifixion brought upon Him the same emotions that we often feel—fear, trepidation, and uncertainty; but each one was offset by His unconquerable desire to set the world free from sin. He was invincibly valorous when it mattered the most, powerfully strong in the face of His adversaries, and absolutely convinced that the reason for His earthly life was being ordained and ratified for the glorification of His Omnipotent Father that day.

It is quite grievous that not every soul He died to save on the Cross has begun the inexorable march toward denying themselves in His image and likeness, and that many in our ranks will never believe in the journey toward spiritual perfection until moments before they expire. In doing so, they are rejecting the connection that Christ has made between the Divinity of God and human Love as we are to share it between ourselves; the laser-beam of revealing Light that connects Heaven and Earth like an umbilical life-line. The Cross is the shortest distance between the Throne of God and the mortal ground on which we walk today; and the Holy Gospel is our intelligible means of communicating with the Paradise we cannot yet see. It would be very difficult for anyone to overstate the significant effect that our openness to this revelation would have on America to the amelioration of our spiritual deficiencies and in reparation for our graves offenses against the Holy Spirit and our own chastity. This is why it is so important for us to refer our children's attention to the Christian Gospel as it is so accurately described in the Catholic Catechism. We sometimes wonder whether the secular world is competing for their attention as an anonymous vendor, or if there is a precisely premeditated agenda at hand by which marketers and corporate moguls are deliberately trying to keep them away from knowing God any better on purpose; the latter being their means of keeping them addicted to such solicitous materialism. We continue to rotate our wares and monitor our checking accounts, nonetheless, assuming that the Truth will eventually discover us if God really cares that much about our living in accordance with it. Our misperception has left our search for morality almost dead in the water because we live in a world that is burdened with such a tenacious and vociferous vogue. However, there is nothing to stop us from deploying this same tactic against itself in an effort to return the world to the center of all spiritual economy; away from the grayish fringes of banality and fashioned ineptitude. To put it more plainly, humanity is gliding asleep when we should be soaring awake, coasting along instead of accelerating aloft, and slouching in our ecclesiastical posture when we should be poised at attention before the mandate of our Divine Lord to do better with our faith. There are certainly many giants among us who have lived and died, and others who remain with us in body and soul that God has positioned in our midst to lead us to His Sacred Kingdom—the Pope John Pauls, Mother Teresas, Jimmy Carters, and Reverend Billy Grahams of the modern world. Let nary a soul believe that he has not the capacity to be just as nobly humble as these!—for there are extenuations to nearly every circumstance. Do we remember, if *i* comes before *e* except after *c*, then how do we explain the word *leisure*? If a human being is walking the face of the Earth with even so much as a sliver of ability to determine right from wrong, then he is capable of understanding, embracing, and reveling the Kingdom of God wherever he should travel. Others who have yet to accept their portion of humankind's responsible nature and spiritual intellect are still innocent bystanders in the judgment of Christ because He has not concluded the world in which they live. Let there be no mistake because He will call upon them before He is through!

Coming to grips with our fragileness is not a losing battle unless we fall into the precarious predicament of wrongly believing that we can thwart the crevasses of mortal life without God's help. Again, we each have a part to play in knowing the reasons why this might occur. As American citizens, how can we expect nonChristians and other nondenominational sectors of the world to understand the Messianic Doctrine of Jesus Christ if we refuse to elevate Him enough to be seen broaching the spiritual horizon between our confluent shores? We will be better able to lift Him up if we allow the heart-strung orchestrations of our pious reflections to touch them where it matters the most—in the heart of their hearts, to which everyone around us must turn for their communion in the very soul of the Mystical Body of Christ. Both supreme prescience and accidental utopia will fall short of captivating our awareness of what the future will bring unless we return to the summits of paradisial holiness like eagles perched atop a precipice or epaulettes sewn permanently on the shoulders of the uniform of spiritual heroism from which we can perceive the *best* of humankind; not only for the proverbial "all seasons," but for the climax of Eternity, itself. There is not a five-star general who ever lived who would not tell us that our thoughts and intentions are only invisible concepts unless we transform them into forcible revelations and discernable action. *What would it be like living in a world where such charity and Love prevailed?* First of all, there is not so much as a kernel of Truth in the assumption that it could never be achieved by us, and only a few shreds of evidence that the majority of the billions of souls who have inhabited the Earth since the fall of man from Heaven have ever really tried. We will get there when we finally understand that there is a certain romanticism in the Sacred Heart of Jesus Christ that people like Emerson and his counterparts could not bring themselves to understand; a Divine Love which has nothing to do with human infatuation with the metaphysical world, but of an appreciation for the keenness of the Cross in Creation, its mystique, the contemplative aspects of its salvific power, and the intrinsically charismatic reflection it has left on the Earth. If we think about all the larger-than-life men and women who have marched across the stage of human achievement, the single attribute they had in common was that they were never quite satisfied with the status quo; their spirits yearned for something greater than to stand idly-by in the shadows and watch their lives expire a day at a time like grains of sand falling off a rock that could not each be uniquely identified one from the next. There lived inside them the explorative heart of an almost sacred ingenuity that was begging to be released into the ignorance of the world.

In the midst of it all, we are a people of good fortune and extremely bad habits, unorthodox and psychopathic rituals, and strange international customs who have arrived at the peak of the world's greatest plateaus replete with unnumerable idiosyncrasies; but we have overcome them by surprising even ourselves as to how original and creative we can be. One might wonder why we have such a knack for clinging to every catch-phrase and slogan that happens to come along when there is such a creative spirit living inside our genes. The reason is rather simple—we are trying to be persuasive in teaching the rest of the world what we have come to know about the environment and our own productivity; and repetition is the key to educating them. I discovered the effect of the lack of such frequency when I was sitting in a doctor's office one time and heard my physician asking a nurse to hand him a tongue depressor from a container that was next to the *sphygmomanometer* on the wall behind her. Little did I know that he was referring to the blood pressure cuff. There is no doubt that we can be as complex in our approach to daily life as we are overly simplistic at times. Our best inclination is to be comfortably childlike in a spiritually mature way; for this is when we begin to see the correlation between a kind heart and good will, common sense and social progress, and personal purity and peace of mind. It is easier for us to recognize thereafter that human Love is our bridge across the cavernous unknowns of the physical universe and the ultimate destiny for which we must strive as our purpose in life. Each of us is conceived with an internal metronome in our being that keeps us in rhythm with the pulse of God, wherein we learn that it is not so much the mechanical function of the heart that matters most, but whether our lives from within it are in sync with the directives of His Will. Our days are overflowing with unseen rainbows and unwritten repertoires; and through our inquisitive nature, we constantly investigate, interrogate, instigate, subjugate, and desecrate the viability of the livelihood of other men. We oftentimes crave lofty things, but are hesitant to elevate the spiritual nature of the functioning of our own existence. We keep looking into the sky as though it is *really* about to fall—all of this while our judicious curiosity and misguided reprisals take the world and its inhabitants to no greater degree of understanding Divine Love. We search far and wide to create a personal identity that rarely, if ever, lives beyond the dusk of the day on which it was spawned; after which we set out to animate another personae altogether to get us through the night. And, what are we learning in the process? That we are still enslaved by the assumption that it costs absolutely nothing to allow our most precious virtues to become extinct, while ceremoniously watching our best potential for Christian holiness unravel before the rest of Creation. There is no alternative for the human race than to turn back to God if our intention is to anticipate a higher calling for living and dying on this transient Earth of ours.

Distractions? What can we say when the American Civil Liberties Union (ACLU) is overly concerned that a first-grader in the back of a public school classroom in Pittsburgh somewhere who is reciting the *Hail Mary* is too pervasively religious for our Western system of democracy, while other people are up to their eyebrows trying to measure the illuminating albedo of the planet Venus to the nearest hundredth of a percent; our tenors and baritones are being coaxed away from the Vienna choir by the ranting of a hurdy-gurdy in some summertime circus, and thousands of people are yielding-back the balance of their time to their surviving spouses by slowly taking their own lives using illicit chemicals and drugs, smoking cigarettes, and binge-drinking alcoholic beverages; or by killing themselves outright with .357 Magnum handguns or running to the top of the nearest high-rise apartment building and throwing themselves off the balcony of the fifteenth floor? *Please bear with me: I am slowly but surely citing the reasons why we are not yet living in a nation that is likely to allow charity and Love to prevail!* Are we better able to discern the necessity of the Church more clearly when we see the results of a humanity that is trying to live devoid of life's purpose? Why can we not see that God is as near to us now through the Holy Spirit as He shall be when we see His Glorious Face? There are people who fly in airplanes that look down at automobiles traveling along the freeway which look like ants crawling across the ground and errantly assume that this is as close as He gets to scrutinizing our everyday world or identifying with the details of our problems and difficulties. It is more suitable for us to remember that He is wholly aware of the inflection of our conversations before we ever conduct them; He knows what issues we will confront today, tomorrow, and next week; and He fully anticipates in advance whether we will be successful in dealing with them. This entire discussion revolves around the fact that we are a diversified people of great complexity, pageantry, and drama; and we fail to see the simpler purposes of life because of the multiple trials and complications we have heaped upon ourselves. When it was said that we cannot see the forest for the trees, it would be more appropriate to say that we are unable to focus upon the Cross because we are so busy contending with the crosses we have created on our own. However, if we become self-sacrificing in a more spiritual way, we will know that only by training our attention upon the needs of those who suffer through our charitable giving will we be able to also heal ourselves. This is the beginning of the prevalence of Love as it is held in such esteem by the Most Blessed Trinity of our sovereign God. The frank imperativeness of our need to return to Him is being slowly lost to us because we are still meandering through the woods of our own pride and defiance in assuming that we can survive the perils of our impending deaths without His supernatural help. On the contrary, only the Love of Jesus Christ can survive as the *genius* and *practical power* that Emerson was seeking all along—the genius of Love and the practical power of shared Christian charity.

We assume that a candle which would be representative of the life of a man that has had the longest time to burn would be the smallest on the altar; but the longer we live, the brighter we become, the more prominent is his grace, emitting a higher light, and the taller we stand in the sight of a very grateful God. This bolsters the reason why we should search for new Christians who can foster fresh energy into an age-old Truth of Mystical Salvation. We are everyone blessed and commended in Jesus for being a chosen race, a royal priesthood, a family of nations, and a people set apart. It has been said for centuries that you can extract more of the best from humankind with honey rather than vinegar; and sweet is the bitterness of the Truth to those who choose to live in accordance with God's Divine Law. We are considered to be imaginative conceivers and grandiose believers whose emphases and impulses are a product of the parameters of our inner-vision; or is this not what Sigmund Freud meant when he originated the concepts of pathos, ethos, and eroticism? The fact is, we are much too disinclined to curb our inhibitions and take the enemies of Love head-on; chocking the wheels of our emotions and defying the way we are absolutely loath to get our hands dirty at times. It is the phantom remnant of some dark-spirited mythology which maintains that everyone must face their worst enemies with cowardice and destroy the devotions we once held for our friends from whence we learned the stories about Jesus together as little children. If only we could grab onto the fashions of our faith that make us common with the early Christians, no adversary of Love will ever succeed in driving a wedge between our hearts again. We should remember that the Catholic Church will never become extinct because it is not subject to the cultural changes that accompany the secular world. Throughout history, the Earth's population has passed-away, one soul at a time; each one taking with them their defining characteristics from the matrix of the present day. After several years, when another generation has come and gone, packing with them the identity of their own times, their vestige is also supplanted by the designs of a new culture that is attributable to their successors—each and every one a product of their environment. This type of evolution *cannot* happen to the Sacraments of the Church because God is the unchanging source of their stationed identity. What we consider to be the "outer years" of the scope of contemporary secularism cannot effect the permanence of His Divine manifestations. This is the constancy of Love that encapsulates the unalterable Truth; and it transpires when and wherever God chooses to reveal another dimension of His original deposit of created life. It is only the effect of His power that mortal men are capable of recording in their theological history books, biographies of the Saints, and their own personal diaries.

Jesus Christ is fully aware of the quarters in His Kingdom that are standing aright and others that we here on Earth have tried to whittle away into something more ignoble than He would like to see. Our Lord is in complete charge of the whole of Creation from its beginning to the end of the world, and everything that we see day-to-day in between. Again, what is our response to the Virgin Mary when the United States stands accused by God of developing our civilization on the back of our own decision to defy the very existence of He who has given us life? Let it be known far and wide that His Judgments carry a much more eternal consequence than the ones rendered by the International Court of Justice near the North Sea in The Hague, Netherlands. Since we do, indeed, consider ourselves to be godless sometimes, are we not depriving ourselves of the Divine Love and prevailing charity of Christ's Supreme Sacrifice on the Cross? Is He not by its power calling us back to the original Apostolic, Catholic Church that He founded and placed under the Papacy of the Pope in Rome? It is only by our participation in the Church that we can be reconciled to God; and His loyal subjects who are His priests are the ministers of this grace. Are not charity and Love surely more than the mere pittance of a meaning to which we have already defined-them-down? Are the current limits of almsgiving, benevolent action, consolation, and benignity the extent to which we are willing to sacrifice ourselves for the King of the world who is so profoundly disguised in the poor? Are we not required to join their poverty by selling what we own and proffering it for feeding them, too? Indeed, what about *Love*? Are we going to accept the skewed concepts of shocking inductive reactance and angular frequencies that those who worship the lightning would have us believe as being our god and creator of life? Divine Love is more than passionate affection or a desire for the fulfillment of the self. It is not constrained to the amour that is espoused by the ancients Eros and Cupid, or a passing predilection and yearning for some strangely forbidden fruit. Reverence and respect are equally insufficient terms with which to describe the totality of the Sovereign Love who has created both Heaven and Earth. The kine and goats feeding upon our greenland pastures cannot produce the same mother's milk with which we are nourished by the very essence of the

Creator of life from whom all good things come. This is why we are supposed to openly avow the stellar perfection of Jesus Christ inside us, reaching for a deeper devotion to the unseen and unexplained; stooping in adoration and worship of the Maker and sustainer of all things benign, and remaining true in consecration to the grace by which we are reclaimed into Paradisial Eternity once again. Our holiness will prevail only by our participation in, identity with, and agreement to the principles of the Divine and supernatural. And, this is from where our Catholic priests procure their ministerial role and authority, at the hands of the Holy Spirit in offering the Seven Sacraments to the Mystical Body of Christ. Our Lord is advancing His Kingdom by purifying us; and in these holy men are we absolved by His Father in the virtuous offices of their sacred ordination. We now own the means for being cleansed and delivered back to the innocence in which Adam and Eve were created. There is no doubt that Heaven has a great deal to say to humanity through the gift of the Roman Catholic Church; and 21st century America stands to benefit more than any other republic from God's present willingness to speak.

Signs from Heaven may not always be seen scrawled on the floor, by a hand writing on the wall, a rose blooming from someone's chest, or anything else we might be able to see or hear with our eyes and ears. But, having previously mentioned poets, philosophers, doctors, psychoanalysts, the devaluing of our cultural decency, emotional derangement, sharing our commodities, and the vital role of the Catechism in amending and effecting all of these; let us not forget that *we are* the Church here on Earth, along with those suffering in Purgatory, and the Saints in Heaven. We can refer to the Eternal Firmament all we want, to suffering and Hell, the stars and moon, the continents and seas, and to the clouds, winds, and skies, as well; but none of these is as important as... *Thy Kingdom come, Thy Will be done*, which is to live at the intersection of our conscience and heart—the latter being that which feeds our thoughts and actions. Love is very simply Love; and human survival is not a matter of the availability of the faculties we require to succeed in the conquest of the higher universe or of our fellow countrymen. What is most important, however, is the strength we should muster to be holy once again and the Wisdom we retain to ensure our safe arrival into the next new world. This is what brought the many hapless Romantics and lyricists to pen their thoughts and affix their hopes to various anthologies of scripted artifacts. Do we suppose they were writing about us, too? Was their purpose to delineate the architecture of their sentiments, hopes, and dreams on a written page because there were too many of them to behold inside their minds at once?

Did they somehow believe that God would read their lofty works along with the rest of our own someday? All of these are probably affirmative assumptions because the curiosity of the Holy Spirit will not allow any well-intentioned argument in His favor or tone of good will to lay undisclosed in the cellar of Creation for very long. It is not fossils and bones we should be exhuming nowadays, but the rare works of the genius of our fathers who accepted Jesus Christ as the Savior of their souls; our authors, teachers, and subscribers who once hailed the Christian dogmas as the true meaning of life. Our cognitive allegiance to God is the entire driving force behind the composite development of the human spirit and the composure we should be carrying when Jesus comes again in Glory. Once the great Milky Way galaxy in which we are situated is fully examined down to the smallest brass tacks of its intrinsic core, our successors will ultimately discover that there was never any other purpose to life than for humankind to worship God, imitate the teachings of His Sacrificed Son, be responsible stewards of the spherical globe on which we live, and listen like spies in the woodwork to the advice and admonishments of the Holy Spirit in our daily chores. We will never conjugate our unity with Paradise unless we conduct ourselves like the Saints who are already living there. This is why our prayerful meditations must be larger than the circumstances which brought us to enter into them from the first moment we discovered that God was quietly listening to us.

Jesus came to purify the men of His age and, by the power of the Cross, He bled this same renewal over into every succeeding generation; complete and indivisible through the conclusion of mortal time. We do not yet own tomorrow because we have not afforded God the opportunity to teach us how to transcend today. He understands that the world is much too segregated right now for Him to have a fighting chance. However, we must never allow the rancor, impurity, and acrimony that is so much a product of the modern secular world to infiltrate the Church any farther than it already has. Our Divine Lord was born, died, and was raised from the Tomb on the Third Day; and He has certainly not left the Earth in the same condition that it was when He entered it. While we are persistently looking for those elusive signs of His presence—playing tricks and gaming with the numbers three, seven, eleven, and 33; the meaning of the world has always been to be much more spontaneously functional than that. It was also supposed to have grown beyond the throes of politics, lust, controversy, tragedy, and entertainment long before we have by now. Innocent people should not be forced to have to spend their days dodging bullets flying through the air, waiting in fear for the other shoe to drop, or plugging the holes in the keel of our social integrity that others have blown into it with their irresponsible indignation to keep our ship of civilization afloat. The Catholic Church is the mitigation over all these ills, and her priests are the living mediators through which she is succeeding. It is by their prompting that humankind is taught to avoid sin in all forms because it separates us from God and is the reason for every source of unhappiness on Earth. His Eminence, Reverend Father Joseph Ratzinger, the renowned theologian and Cardinal Prefect of the Sacred Congregation for the Doctrine of the Faith, which is a curial office in Rome, once gave an interview to writer and journalist Vittorio Messori that was excerpted into a published book entitled *The Ratzinger Report* (Ignatius Press, San Francisco 1985), in which he discusses the state of the Church in the latter decades of the 20th century; specifically our need to return to the faithful promises that the early Church made to God by its enforcement of the Truth and keeping with His statutes and Commandments; much in contrast to our secular world today. *"...the more one understands the holiness of God, the more one understands the opposite of what is holy, namely, the deceptive masks of the devil. Jesus Christ, Himself, is the greatest example of this: before Him, the Holy One, Satan could not keep hidden and was constantly compelled to show himself. So, one might say that the disappearance of the awareness of the demonic indicates a related decline in holiness. The devil can take refuge in his favorite element, anonymity, if he is not exposed by the radiance of a person who is united to Christ...Anyone who has a clear picture of the dark sides of the age in which we live sees forces at work which aim to disintegrate the relationships among men. In this situation, the Christian can see that his task as exorcist must regain the importance it had when the faith was at its beginning. Of course, the word 'exorcism' must not be understood here in its technical sense; it simply refers to the attitude of faith as a whole, which 'overcomes the world' and 'casts out' the prince of this world. Once the Christian has begun to be aware of this dark abyss, he knows that he owes the world this service. Let us not succumb to the popular idea that 'we can solve all problems with a little good will.' Even if we did not have faith, but were genuine realists, we would be convinced that, without the assistance of a higher power—which, for the Christian, is the Lord alone—we are prisoners of a baneful history. If we remain united to Christ, we can be sure of victory...If we look closely at the most recent secular culture, we see how the easy, naive optimism is turning into its opposite—radical pessimism and despairing nihilism. So it may be that the Christians who up to now were accused of being 'pessimists' must help their brothers to escape from this despair by putting before them the radical optimism which does not deceive—whose name is Jesus Christ."* (pp. 148-149).

Hence, we have a more humane way to approach the rest of the world with a sense of higher reasoning and comprehensive responsiveness with which the confounded and bewildered among us can identify. What Cardinal Ratzinger is extolling is that our helplessness before God does not infer that we cannot be triumphant in defeating Satan because we are living members of the Roman Catholic Church. By all means, his words revel the supernatural power that comes to us through the guidance of the Holy Spirit. His priestly affirmations are no accident as they are compelling evidence of the strength of the Love inside the human heart. We can warn the enemies of our Salvation that we intend to become all that God asks us to be, but it is only through our own prayerful, spiritual, and Christological imitation of Jesus that it can be done. Such faith is not something we are required to be taught in a formal classroom-setting somewhere to put into practice because we rarely, if ever, hear the ringing of a bell when the Holy Paraclete enters our heart. After all, we learned to walk as infant children long before we were ever fitted with shoes; and even thereafter, the maturity of our development has left us anything but static in the prolificness of our growth. All evangelical power is a fused and amalgamated conjoining of the natural and the paranormal. We do not have to look very far to discover the evidence because we are treading along the pathways of life in the shadows of some of the greatest spiritual heroes of any age; many of them who have been appropriately called "earth-angels" in their own right, who wielded a Divine prowess for understanding the Love of God that would bring tears of happiness to the eyes of the most callous among men. Their Laudatory refrains and Gregorian Chants were music to the expectancy of the same Christ who encouraged them; their songs and liturgies a reminder to everyone in their wake that Love has touched the world-entire; morning, noon, and night. Surely the original Apostles and the Saints of our latter times have become the bookends which keep the volumes of God's deigned affection for humanity upright before the permeable history of all previous histories. They have also left us uncharted trails to blaze, as well, with the mightiness of the swords of His ingenious propriety that they carefully honed to razor-like perfection with the guttural grittiness of their allegiance to Christ. As Emerson said, the element of time can truly fool us when we are not paying close attention to its rite of passage. When we look up into the midnight sky and see a 747 jet airliner passing across the silvery glow of the moon, we can imagine what the world might have thought of such a sight in the first century after Jesus' birth. And, yet, He knew from the start that we would be standing in the darkness 2,000 years later, peering at the same moon under which He tread many times before, as a child who played in the dooryard with His Mother Mary, His stepfather Joseph, and perhaps a friend or two who lived nearby. Do we suppose He told them back then about the modern industrial and technological advances that we are enjoying today? Indeed, would anyone outside His family and circle of disciples have believed Him anyway? And, yet, we drive past our airports everyday and think nothing about it, just as He thought we would do 2,000 years ago in the annals of recorded time. The point I am making is that there is no difference in the notable prescience that Our Lord wielded in His mortal days and the signature of grace under which His priests are living now; not that they can predict the future with the pinpoint accuracy of a needle and thread; but that they are aware of the possibility that the very essence of our existence on the Earth can be transformed by God into something entirely unrecognizable to civilized humankind in the matter of an instantaneous flash.

Our priests may not be capable of telling us what might appear in the night skies in A.D. 4000, should there be such a year; but they are just as close to God, endearing to the intentions of His Will, subject to the same tests of their faith, and owning the mysterious capacity to utter the words of consecration at any moment in time and facilitate the transubstantiation of the gifts of bread and wine into the Eucharistic Species of the very Son of God who died on the Cross to save us. The stark difference is that they are beyond any doubt all sinners, while Jesus was perfectly sinless in every facet that could possibly be conceived. This is why we must continue to pray for them, so they will be confident in their mission, resilient in their suffering, and proactively compassionate toward grieving humankind in the likeness of the Lord. I once heard a Protestant college classmate tell me that if he believed the Most Blessed Sacrament to be the Body and Blood of Jesus Christ, *he* would convert to Catholicism and apply for entrance into the seminary to become a priest, himself. My response was that our faith is more subliminal than that; and God would call him into the vocation if it was in accordance with His Will. As for my classmate's reluctance to believe in the real presence of Jesus Christ in the Holy Eucharist; his soul, his life, his family, our nation, the world, and the entire of Creation are the poorer for his lack of faith. We are not summoned to the Table of the Lord like fish searching for a worm wiggling on a hook; for *we* are the fishers of men with the largesse of our trust in God, multiplied many thousands of times over again, and seeping from within the holy-saturated chambers of our sanctified hearts into the parched remains of an unconverted Earth. Perhaps the coveys of Seraphim Angels might be more than willing to offer their pretty processionals to such an event if more of us would afford them a reason and the proper opportunity. They hover just overhead when we are sitting alone in a wooded countryside after dusk and hear the chirping crickets, crooning bullfrogs, the wind sailing through the branches of the evergreen trees, and the distant howl of a prairie dog; and they whisper into our hearts in agreement with our confidence that everything is right with Nature in the smaller "world" to which we have become attuned. But, realizing that we cannot stay their forever, and soon will come the dawn; we are urged by the Holy Spirit to awaken again, sent back into the work of our hands and the motivations of our hearts that will heal the world of its agony and deceit. Are not such occasions as these our parables to the respites we take inside the recitation of our prayers, where our motivations can be as immense and important as the entire study of angelology has become to the charismatic theologians of our age?

We are not required to become cloistered ascetics to remain this closely united to God in our petitions because He draws no distinctions between our souls and the Hosts of Paradise once we have tendered them to His Son. When the world around us seems to be bursting at the seams with vengeance, anger, and indignation, we can always turn our hearts to Him as a voluntary affirmation to His invitation to become united as one inside His eternal peace. The unseen part of Creation is always unfazed and undaunted by the perils of the world because the Holy Trinity lives there in perfect tranquility; the same generous serenity Jesus often gave to those who needed to be consoled in the precincts where He lived as a carpenter's Son being reared in the humble confines of Nazareth. Believe it now or rue our defiance; we can be so obstinate against this Truth that we would risk the everlasting fate to which our spirits are destined to remain. It is sometimes difficult to believe that God would allow a departed soul to endure the agony of spiritual ruin inside the grotesque warehouse of the damned within the utter destruction of Hell. That is why He remands the decision to be *ours* to make; and He allows it by the invocation of the crest of Truth upon our deceased soul the very moment we die. Can we say that we would wilfully choose to consider ourselves worthy for admittance into Paradise just the way we are? Are there certain people around us now who would be as happy to know that they made it into the "temporary haven" of Purgatory when it comes their time to go? After all, it can be quite a gruesome place of suffering on its own! This is not the higher hope in which our conversion was meant to be unfolded. When Jesus Christ said, *"...be perfect, as I am perfect,"* He was not telling us to take a notation for a later course of amendment sometime in the distant future; but He means here and now, waiting not a moment longer to reconcile with His Father who is sitting in wait high above the Earth on His sovereign Throne. It is true that there are countless people who have not received the Sacrament of Confession in over twenty-five years, but God will forgive them for all the times in between if they offer Him a good examination of their conscience, repent of their sinfulness, perform a good act of contrition, and promise to amend the way they live. And, until each one of us does so, our very future is suspended in doubt inside a dark mausoleum of guilt and shame that is of our own manufacturing. Our spirits lay in waste and stagnant disgrace until we finally decide to make lasting peace with our Creator and regain our spiritual dignity again.

Our priests are in-service for the expressed purpose of closing the fissure between humankind and God; and Heaven responds both instantly and emphatically to us by bridging that same rift with discernable signals and portative graces that we carry at the center of our being wherever we go. The Catholic clergy are God's holy instruments who are literally vested with Christ's full authority to speak on His behalf in offering the quittance we require to judge ourselves with as great a pity and humble pardon as He is apt to do. His robed "little emmanuels" grant us a wholly Sacramental vindication from our incarceration inside our sins; not that they are by any means to be hailed as equals to the only true Messiah; but because they are His mortal witnesses and couriers who proclaim with His full commission that the Son of God is here and our eternal Salvation is nigh at hand. The Sacred Nuptials between the Roman Catholic Church and Jesus Christ, Himself, will be the most grand affair that Creation has ever seen; and His charity and Love will fully prevail without a dissenting ballot from the Earth or the lofty Halls of Paradise. Does it seem nearly impossible that the Almighty Father would allow His Sacrificed Son to take humanity's hand in marriage after all we have done to spurn His courtship over the past twenty centuries? What kind of a world would force the only perfect Man to be born to go from the Creche to the Cross because of the spreading of Good News that He did not begin to impart to humankind until thirty-six months before He was put to death? It seems as though we are only now beginning to recognize that the Glorious power of God's forgiveness was never really limited to the incarnate frame in which He chose to appear on the Earth as His only begotten Son. He was born a child and raised to the age of thirty-three years before He was impaled to the Cross on a desolate Hill in the Middle East, but He is also a timeless Martyr for all generations; and in Him continues to live the little child in the best of us, the innocuous playfulness of a Babe in His Mother's Arms, a strapping young adolescent of quick wit and soft charm, a wise scholar of spiritual Truth, and a learned gentleman of ministerial maturity. Yet, He was still simply God, willing to drape Himself in the Flesh of a plain and ordinary Man; except during His Transfiguration before Peter, James, and John; so as to teach humanity how to live, pray, serve, confide, and hope. Do we dare harbor the audacity to stumble through life with our hands flailing through the air in wonderment about a world and a universe which can neither one grant us the solemnity and peace for which human hearts have longed for tens-of-thousands of years? Are we so filled with defeatism that we would crawl into a hole in the ground as deep as the height of Mount Tabor, itself, and proclaim before Creation that we cannot be transfigured, too, by a manifest Salvation that has everything to do with the Crucifixion of Christ? God might allow us to be so bold as to presume that another reason that Jesus declined the invitation of His Apostles to erect booths that day was because He feared there may have been an insufficient amount of materials left in the world to construct the coffins to contain the remains of the untold number of souls who would eventually reject their Redemption in Him all the way to the present hour in which we are living. Our death is getting nearer; but so is our rising from the grave in His Resurrection. Let us all go out to greet Him with our Baptismal garments unstained and lighted lamps in hand; together in the company of the Angels and Saints when God recommends that the fullness of time has arrived.

Section Three
Go Make of All Disciples

Chapter IX
Life, Love, and Hypostasis

"...later, as the eleven were at table, He appeared to them and rebuked them for their unbelief and hardness of heart because they had not believed those who saw Him after He had been raised. He said to them, 'Go into the whole world and proclaim the Gospel to every creature. Whoever believes and is baptized will be saved; whoever does not believe will be condemned. These signs will accompany those who believe: in My Name they will drive out demons; they will speak new languages. They will pick-up serpents with their hands, and if they drink any deadly thing, it will not harm them. They will lay hands on the sick, and they will recover. You are witnesses of these things; and behold, I am sending the promise of My Father upon you. All power in Heaven and on Earth has been given to Me. Go, therefore, and make disciples of all nations, baptizing them in the Name of the Father, and of the Son, and of the Holy Spirit; teaching them to observe all I have commanded you. And, behold, I am with you always, until the end of the age.' There are also many other things that Jesus did, but if these were to be described individually, I do not think the whole world would contain the books that would be written."

> *The Gospel of the New Covenant*
> SS Matthew 28: 18-20
> Mark 16: 14-18
> Luke 24: 48-49
> John 21: 24-25

If our religious discussion is going to be germane to the pertinent issues that are confronting the Catholic Church today, it would be wholly inappropriate if we failed to include the matters over which we, ourselves, as lay-persons have the capacity to ameliorate. If there appears to be an even slightly evident degeneracy in the reputation of modern Christianity; and specifically the Roman Catholic Church, it is the direct result of our own unwillingness to declare its power strongly or convincingly enough for our enemies to desist in their onslaught. It is almost as though God has founded a fashionable fortress that is designed by His grace to be a hundred times taller than the Statue of Liberty, an immeasurable degree more beautiful than the Austrian Alps, and as evocative to the soul as the speeches that are hewn in stone and etched onto gold tablets on the Lincoln and Washington Monuments in the District of Columbia. In all her sovereign majesty, the Catholic Church is near the summit of Her perfected state; but it is upon the smallest crack in its decor that our adversaries have chosen to concentrate. Never mind, they say, that a soul would have to stand in a distant universe to discern a panoramic view of its holiness; or place a welder's mask before their eyes to permeate its irreproachable Light, or ask the likes of Saint Thomas Aquinas, himself, what the indescribable gift of Divine Love really means. While we are not presupposed to be delusional about the gravity of our mistakes, there are certain people surrounding the phenomenon of Christianity only because they are feeding upon the current frenzy about our internal problems. In ancient Greece, the term "parasite" was used to describe someone who often received free meals in return for his amusing conversation. In 21ˢᵗ century America, however, it refers to the clowns and heretics who are searching for the slightest breach in the Church's spiritual hull, at which point they will attempt to drive a wedge of theological cynicism more deeply therein to try to get it to founder. No one should forget that the Catholic Church is the world's felicitous source of all dogmatic Revelation in its finest hour; and no man who is either dead or alive has the authority to amend its sacred purpose without the direct and concise intercession of the Holy Spirit of God; and only then through the Seat of Christianity, the occupant of the Chair of St. Peter at the Vatican in Rome. The purpose of entering the Church is two-fold: that our personal spiritual Salvation may be secured, and so the Church as the instrument of the Redemption of humankind might continue to flourish through the faithful participation of our children in our own pious works.

If someone converts to Christianity and is thereafter disconcerted by how its mission is being accomplished, he is required to redress his grievances from within it; ensuring that we help the Church remain under the guidance of Jesus Christ by summoning His assistance as one body in Him. Let there be no confusion; anyone that professes to be a Christian in the likeness of the Saints who wilfully engages an outside, secular source for the resolution of their complaints is turning their back on the Cross, walking away from His righteous hope, and committing blasphemy against the very originative power and Divine grace by which all Creation is healed. There are some among us who will resort to reading palms and tea leaves while looking for answers;

others who stare into a crystal ball, decipher the meaning of tarot cards, or study the arrangement of the stars in an attempt to "divine" the fate of the future. None of these is a legitimate source of Christian Truth, but they are no more fallacious in solving our ecclesiastical problems than those who are clad in jurists' robes in public courtrooms, people who wear badges and carry guns, or men and women who pore over the files in our national archives, searching for the meaning of life. From the perspective of the Divine autonomy of Jesus Christ, we are subject to His indictments as well as His absolutions; and He is the only Master whom the entire world must serve; not a democratic institution or a flag of pragmatic colors, and not our patriotic songs that mention His Name only in passing. There is not a scintilla of evidence in the Holy Bible to confirm that God has ever shed His grace on the United States. So, why do we assume that He has? Could it be by reason of our having the good fortune to own the greatest military arsenal in the history of the world with which we regularly threaten any outside entity that might deem it appropriate to address our obvious international parsimony? Has humanity ever known the blessing of God to be dispensed upon a nation that dropped an atomic weapon on Hiroshima, Japan on August 6, 1945 and a second one on the city of Nagasaki three days later; effectively killing, maiming, burning, and scarring hundreds of thousands of people in the name of military revenge? Do we ever see supple rose petals dropping from the skies at the urging of the Blessed Mother of God in our largest American cities within inches of their Planned Parenthood abortion clinics?

If we believe that our source of freedom is the commendation or ratification by God of our historical legacy and personal lifestyles, we had better take another serious look at what it means to be "free." Our social economy is filled with so many incidental and farcical predicaments and bawdy coincidences that are many times the work of the devil that even the low-comedy of his sorcerers is no longer amusing to the damned. On the other hand, the truly inspired children of God can detect the signature of perfect Love because we are in the business of professing it. If there are occasions when certain events occur simultaneously, or on an exact date in different years; if they correspond in substance and effect, or coincide in any other way, God will tell us by the particular fruits they bear whether His Divine Will is involved and everything else is according to Hoyle. We must be very wary about the ability of Satan to mock the good will of decent men for the purpose of leading them astray and far from the Sacraments of the Church. This is yet another precise description of the circumstances where public officials and sworn enemies of Catholicism are appearing in woolen sweaters and cranky neckties, carrying black brief-cases with summonses enclosed, who claim they have come to "rescue" various parishioners that have been the unfortunate targets of the weaknesses of other Christians. To set the record straight: there is no such thing as being rescued *from* the Church in any sense of the term. If there are occasions when our Christian counterparts exude an unwholesome, seamy, offensive, or mordant attitude or conduct toward anyone in their midst or under their ministerial care, the time has come to rescue *them* from the grisly grasp of Satan's jaws. It is a matter of factual course that those they have victimized and scandalized must be embraced with compassion, consolation, and healing; but God will never allow us to get-by with throwing their defendants into the dungeon of anyone's vile hatred or treating them like despicable wretches because they have fallen to the temptations of sin in ways that the rest of us would probably not. The prognosis for the beneficial displaying of our Christian charity in forgiving them is not as good when there are galleries of hecklers standing in the mix of an already difficult situation, trying to coax the rest of us into tossing them to the alligators for the sake of some vindictive reprisal. Why would we not, instead, invoke the remedial and reverently applicable intercession of the Son of God in the wake of all this?

To the degree by which we have come to understand the meaning of life and Love, we are required by the tenets of our Catholic profession of faith to comply with the advocacy of the Holy Trinity in time and space, i.e, to grant Jesus Christ both the opportunity and compatible environment to manifest His *hypostasis*, meaning that the vast body of humankind must accord Him plentiful venue to succeed in His commission as the singular Messiah in Creation whose purpose is to unite the human and the Divine. Do we remember His words from Saint Matthew's Gospel?—*"All power in Heaven and on Earth has been given to Me!"* And, if we are to do this in accordance with the stated Will of the Father, with whom Jesus Christ exists as the Second Person of the Trinity, and in unity with the Holy Paraclete as it is so clearly and articulately presented in the Sacred Scriptures; we have no alternative than to cease and desist from prosecuting our fallen priests, return them to the fold in roles where they are not apt to surrender to such temptations again, forget completely about their confessed transgressions, forego any punishment or calls for reparation; financial and otherwise, and move forward together in faith as a chastened group of Christian believers. We have always known that excellent, preeminent, and resplendent is the Wisdom by which humankind is taught right from wrong. Our journey of faith in this valley of tears need not be a burden of blindness or spiritual incapacity because we can clearly see through the broadest definition of Love what Jesus meant when He told the world that we must seek His Father's Kingdom from the center of the heart. Every person on the face of the globe can generate a living sense for this vision because we all own the same capacity to Love; whether we choose to embrace it or not. After all, this is what our Christian conversion is all about. Let us not confuse the search for the meaning of life in the sublime subsistence of God with civil disputes in which some people otherwise find themselves involved. Those whose loyalty belongs to the latter approach the followers of Christianity as though we are carrying some type of curse by which we intend to strip them of their assets, or that we are a collection of claim-jumpers who have arrived at their doorstep demanding the deeds to their lands. The final Truth of the matter is that we who hope in Jesus Christ are delivering the message of God's Eminent Domain which is quickly approaching from just-over the horizon of the next minute; and it is the Holy Spirit who reveals to us how far we stand from being prepared to receive Him. The determining factor as to whether someone is receptive of this enlightenment is how the Gospel is accepted inside their heart. There is no subversion or deception in what Our Lord wants from us because the Holy Scriptures oftentimes reveal His extemporaneous declarations and inclinations in quite candid, terse, and outspoken terms. The purpose of life therein is to return lost souls to the center of Divine Love through the hypostatic intercession of the Son of God who also happened to have paid the price to the satisfaction of His Father for the expiation of our sins. It is important for us to remember hereon that no form of bloodless execution would have sufficed because the Blood of Jesus Christ must continue to flow during the Holy Sacrifice of the Mass to reveal the true and real presence of our Salvation in the modern-day world to the expungement of the sins we commit in our time.

When Jesus took the Cup into His sacred hands in the Upper Room on the night before He died, we are told that it was already filled with wine; thereby stipulating His scripted desire that we are to pour-out our lives, our intentions, and our very souls into the Blessed Chalice within the privacy of our hearts and contemplative thoughts during the Holy Sacrifice of the Mass so as to be in coessential unity with the power of the Cross. It is highly possible and more than probable that Roman Catholics who attend the Eucharistic Celebration on a regular basis are capable of rendering a vision of Creation from *within* the Chalice, itself; which is our discernable reference to the way Our Lord wants us to envision the world through the offering of our self-sacrifices in converting, purifying, and healing humanity in reflection of

His Crucifixion. The conventional character of our living faith is hereafter augmented by the tenor of trust that God gives us during our reception of Holy Communion; and we believe with greater confidence in His Divine assistance from that moment forward; until we attend the Holy Sacrifice again. We are not necessarily "stapled" to the purism of Heaven as though our souls are hemmed to its circumference; rather we are reclaimed as an intrinsic part of its original center, back into compliance with the perfection in which God first gave humanity life. Hence, we are the chieftains, comrades, and constables of an alliteration of expressed religiosity when we sit, kneel, and stand before the Holy Altar to participate in the Crucifixion of Jesus Christ. It is from the Mass that we garner the foresight and strength to be forgiving in the many ways that we are called to do so, and especially now. Christianity is, perhaps, the only battle that has already been won in which we, as God's foot-soldiers, are being called to take-up our arms against wanton hatred and evil after-the-fact. When we are sitting in peaceful contemplation, lifting our prayers for the healing of the world, we are wielding our swords of Truth and firing our cannons with righteous ferocity. While we are ascribing praise to God in perspicuous doxologies, the silent Angels in our midst are doing their greatest work. Indeed, should we call-out for His intervention as an Ecclesial college of self-mortified Christians, Jesus will come running to us with a scepter of emollience in His hands to open a line of communication between Heaven and Earth that rivals both Niagra Falls and the Michigan-Canadian Sault St. Marie rapids.

The optimum moment for proving to the rest of the world that the Roman Catholic Sacraments are the true Graces of Love from the Throne of God has arrived; now, while the memories of absolved offenses are still waning; as those who have been offended are removing the dressing from their deeply-inflicted wounds, and in the meantime during which their trespassers are undergoing an appropriate penance. This is the function of the real, living Church in action; gathering beneath the Cross for strength and consolation in both good times and in bad. The Light of Divine Justice will never dim or grow stale with age; but there is no time like the present for Catholics everywhere to celebrate the Church as an inclusive institution of charismatic professors of Divine inspiration, rather than a collection of flat-line realists who are only going through the motions of explicating the parables of the Scriptures without living them from within. If Christians cannot forgive other Christians, who *can* they forgive? There is no magical potion to drink or pills to pop that will make us mysteriously a more unified people again; for we are asked to do it by the virtues of the very Messianic

Gospel we have proclaimed. The Hosts of Paradise will not descend from above and kiss humanity on the cheek as though we are a pickerel-toad sitting on a sandbar somewhere and instantly change our ugly grudges into a princely consonance. What must be done to reunite the Church and send the predators against us packing, those who are lurking in the wings that are hunting for someone to ridicule and detest, is to clearly show them the cohesive power of Christian pardoning. Despite anything they may try to do to malign the Church, Jesus Christ is not going to bend to their thirst for vengeance by transmuting His lawful engagement with His Mystical Body into something altogether different or cancel our impending wedding banns on the last day of time just to satisfy those who say He should have courted some other species or unknown creature on a planet to which none of us has ever been. When we see scenes that depict two old fogies playing checkers on their back porch or four finely-coifed ladies engaged in a game of Chinese mah-jongg in the dinner parlour, we assume that this is what it will be like to enter our elderly years and have nothing else better to do. Unfortunately, this same Norman Rockwell portrait gives us the wrong impression of what Our Divine Lord is doing now; given the fact that He is over 2,000 years of age and counting. Jesus has always existed in God's Creation because He is, likewise, God. The only frame of reference in which He was influenced by time was when He lived in Incarnate Flesh among us for thirty-three years, twenty centuries ago. Since He is completely ageless and never tires from seeking the Salvation of our souls, He is still alive and present in our midst in the Third Person of the Trinity: the Holy Paraclete; and His reasoning for remaining is that His work is not quite finished yet. Inside our hearts, and through His Sacramental Body, Blood, Soul, and Divinity in the Holy Eucharist, He has taken both refuge and residence in the "being" of His humanity that is still exiled on the Earth. We, therefore, are Jesus' piety in the way we Love, comply with the beatific intension of His scrupulous commands, and become the fleshborne Will of His Father in Heaven for as long as we shall live.

Our Lord has imparted to us the ability to comprehend everything He ever said or did; and if we are reluctant in submitting to any part of it, then are not we the worse sinners of all? Our march toward Paradise will bear a shocking resemblance to tragic news to us someday if we suddenly awaken from our obstinate sleep to discover that it is *our* better conscience, prompted by Christ's Love, that is demanding our return to the point of our original conversion to begin the journey anew. This is what Jesus referred to when He told His disciples that they may be the better judges of their ways and means, after all. He was addressing the fact that God is not going to fall onto His knees before our dearly departed souls when we die and beg us not to condemn ourselves; and this is why it is so gravely important that we comply with the lessons and teachings of His Son today—eliminating the slightest whiff of pride and hypocrisy from the way we conduct our affairs, settling our disputes with judicious prudence, and treating those we wrongfully disdain with respect. His Spirit can see completely beyond the barricaded parameters that separate the secluded boroughs of our sprawling municipalities; so He should have absolutely no difficulty discerning the motivations behind our actions. We cannot hide from Him; nor should we desire to, because all morality and appellate judgment is seated within the power of His Love. We know already that the Earth is comprised of four directions in the shape of a sphere, and it does not have squarely quadratic corners. Is there a parable in this or a metaphor for better understanding our spiritual faith? If we allow Our Savior into our hearts while we are still in mortal flesh, our very daily existence becomes the inverse precision of God. We are to wilfully sow to this Spirit, imitate the unseen, storehouse treasures in a Heaven that is still beyond our vision, and look for Jesus Christ inside the lives of the poor. Indeed, these are tangible aspects of a regenerative Kingdom that is the physical shape of the Cross, with all its angles and corners intact. Therein, we have become the very Love that we espouse through the Divine intervention of an invisible Heaven. If we ever came into contact with someone who fosters the highly rigid suppression of dissident political or ideological views, the concentration of power in a single man or woman, and a paranoically aggressive military foreign policy, then it would be safe to say that we have just met a staunch Stalinist; so named for the secretary general of the Communist party in the USSR from 1922-1953. Could we expect that our identity might be used someday to extol Christianity as a complementary term, as well? After all, a rose by any other name smells as sweet. The point is, we must do more than just give lip-service to the Glory of Christ; we are asked to become the heirs of the faith of the Apostles by living the same conviction that took the majority of them to their violent deaths.

So, now, the proposition of our dedication has begun. Our dear God who has spangled the celestial cosmos with His regal power, idealistic joy, distinctive splendor, royal brilliance, and superb endowment is waiting for us to act and react; to requisition His Divine Mercy, implore His pardon and favor; to feed upon His clemency, conquer world hatred through His meritorious excellence, give freely of our Love in personifying His beauty, charm, and grace; and manifest His simplicity while taking our souls to the summit of the Cross; lest we succumb to the oppressing insurrection that has betided so many prideful souls before us. If our conscience sends us reeling into the hindsight of regret, it is still not too late for us to seek Christ both openly and unreservedly. Let us not deplane from the plateaus of our conversion before we have flown to the starry heights of holiness where reverence lives in perpetuity, forever and a day. Our vigilance in prayer is our precognition that the worst of life has passed-away, and we can hear the pipers echoing down the hallowed avenues of the awesome liberties that are just beyond our grasp. Our Nobel laureates have spoken of disjunction and concordance in single monographs, and how lathes and laws of motion kept Sir Isaac Newton's feet both planted firmly atop the ground; so surely our misanthropic lives will find us in Christ's contempt, or that we might enjoy the mirth of His own amusement if we ever gave Him a chance to laugh. Can we go now, arm-in-arm, toward the Gate that is so steep and narrow, and almost too far away to be seen from the confines of our flesh? Gone are Italy's Fascist Benito Mussolini, the ghosts of Leningrad, Hitler's Nazi socialists, and Herod Antipas; the latter who executed John the Baptist and took part in the trial of Jesus Christ. The world is much more free today, although we still have a long way to go because some of our worst enemies are coming from *within* as we embark on a new millennium; not from the shads and sardines we may have had for lunch, but because of the haunting and hesitating shyness that keeps us from lauding the Holy Name of Christ from the rooftops of our homes. If we stand upon the headland bluffs and look-out over the seas, will we not be able to touch God's horizons of tender majesty? Perhaps the motto of the U.S. Marine Corps would be equally as appropriate in defining our commitment to christening the world in the Love of Paradise—*Semper Fidelis*, is what they proudly proclaim; "always faithful," is their battle cry. We hold the strength to uproot the ruins and the corruption of the world in the power of the Cross, if only we will wield it, and implant the seeds of peace and hope firmly in their place. We shall not discover the greatest courage ever known to humankind in the spoils of our drudgery or conceit; nor will the Light of Christ shine before other men if our sins become their blinders from seeing it for themselves.

O' Christ, the Great Foundation

O' Christ, the Great Foundation
On which your people stand
To preach your true Salvation
In every age and land:
Pour-out your Holy Spirit
To make us strong and pure,
To keep the faith unbroken
As long as worlds endure.   8
Baptized in one confession,
One Church in all the Earth,
We bear our Lord's impression
The Sign of second birth.
One holy people gathered
In love beyond our own,
By grace we were invited,
By grace we make you known.   16
Where tyrants' hold is tightened,
Where strong devour the weak,
Where innocents are frightened,
The righteous fear to speak.
There, let your Church awaking,
Attack the powers of sin,
And, all their ramparts breaking,
With you the Victory win.   24
This is the moment Glorious
When He who once was dead,
Shall lead His Church victorious,
Their champion and their head.
The Lord of all Creation
His Heavenly Kingdom brings
The final consummation,
The Glory of all things!   32

-Timothy T'ingfang Lew (1891-1947)
Christian Conference of Asia

Chapter X
Mary of Bethlehem
The Immaculate Conception

"What will the children of Mary be like in the latter times? They will be like thunder clouds flying through the air at the slightest breath of the Holy Spirit. Attached to nothing, surprised by nothing, troubled at nothing, they will shower down the rain of God's Word and of Eternal Life. They will storm against the world; they will strike down the devil and his followers; and for life or for death, they will pierce through and through with the two-edged sword of God's words all those against whom they are sent by Almighty God."

Saint Louis de Montfort   (1673-1716)
True Devotion to Mary
Chapter I, Article III, Number 57

Alas! God draws the ultimate conclusion to the Sacred Mysteries of His Will by dispatching His Immaculate Mother to be our intercessor before the Savior of the World! Now, we see through Her eyes that the planet on which we reside is not really a kennel filled with vicious dogs that have been sicced upon us by Satan, himself, but a Kingdom of Love and Truth in-the-rough, one that we must embrace with the likes of the very Saints who are praying for us at Her side. For all who are offended, anyone who has fallen into the snake-pit of their sins; to those who are awaiting a response from Heaven as to when or how to grasp for the best of God's blessings—we have found it in the Blessed Virgin Mary. Her intercessory Wisdom has altered the meaning of mortal life for us who are consecrated to Her Immaculate Heart. Her Divine nature enhances the power of our prayers, expands the scope of our spiritual vision, clarifies the purpose of human suffering, magnifies the Glory of Almighty God, reveals the Truth much more distinctly, justifies the repetition of the litanies, intensifies the compassion in our hearts, purifies the essentialness of our pleading, and indemnifies the loss of our dignity by leading us to the Holy Cross of Jesus Christ. Her beaming purposes are nothing-less than directively sublime as She prepares us to mind our mensal manners before the Feast Table of the Lord. Our Lady has helped humanity to redefine our reasoning and has blessed our work for twenty centuries, giving us strength to discharge our duties with the expectation that Her Son is still watching. How the Mother of God wishes that Her children would accept the paradisial peace which we are still defiantly resisting because our will-to-power is stronger than our willingness to Love! If only we could know how the Blessed Mother has placed a renewed emphasis upon the Sacraments of the Roman Catholic Church, we would greet one another inside them for the purpose of never being separated in heart or soul again. She anticipates our acceptance of Her instruction, cooperative understanding, consolation, admonishment, and willingness to persist in the face of the world's reluctance to seek the Heaven where She reigns as Queen. None of these should be diminished by anything foreign, domestic, baneful, whimsical, or indifferent. We must be aware of the piousness of our thoughts that She is still trying to beatify so God above will ordain the tasks at our hands through the unparalleled conviction of His desire for our mutual success.

Our Lady is the Mother of the Church, the Bride of the Holy Spirit, Matron of the Angelic Court, Matriarch of the Communion of Saints, and Patroness of the Americas; and She resounds the resolute requirements for human forgiveness, faithfulness, charity, common sense, and good will. If our focus is, indeed, to be reoriented to the Sacred and the Divine, we must acknowledge Her capacity to change us into the little children about whom Jesus Christ spoke in the Bible. Through the simplicity of Her Immaculate Heart, She exemplifies the perfection of a humbled humanity because She was conceived without sin and has never fallen to the temptations of human arrogance or pride. The Blessed Virgin Mary is the precise reflection of the Divine piousness of the Messiah She bore to save us from the fires of Hell; He who leads all souls to Heaven, especially those who are in most need of His Divine Mercy. There is no question that Our Lady is our model for Christian perseverance, the Seer who augments our spiritual reflections, our Advocate before the Lord's judicious temperament, counsel for the chosen flock of Messianic believers, and guiding refuge for our priests in whom Jesus has bequeathed their vocations. The Blessed Virgin is a prefigured participant in the conversion, cultivation, purifying, and Redemption of all humanity—an active partaker in the deliverance of Her Son's Mystical Body to the foot of the Cross. There is no doubt that Her role is a Divine manifestation in the Church of the Original Catholic Apostles because She is wholly rejected by Protestants, despised to the core by atheists, ignored by pragmatists, ridiculed by realists, and maligned by the secular world as a figment of someone's imagination in the likes of Ruskin's *pathetic fallacy* from Modern Painters in 1856, fit only for worry-warts and eccentric novelty seekers. Even in all of this, She has been preserved by God to be dignified and undefiled. The entire basis of human life should be plotted around Her persistence, and the beatification of the world founded upon Her Love. She implores the womenkind on the Earth to imitate Her grace-filled ways, and for every boy and girl in their fruitful wombs to become "little Christs and little Marys" after they are born. When She tells Her messengers through miraculous apparitions and interior locutions that the Morning of Christ's Return is finally breaking, too many among us respond that we cannot yet hear the birds chirping or see the broaching of the dawn. Her answer is that we are too distracted by the noise of window-shattering music, profane language, and off-color jokes; and we will not look skyward enough to see from where the daylight is springing.

Indeed, how can we hear the mellow voice of the Holy Spirit when there is so much distraction from our bombs exploding in neighborhood streets, the squalls of scathing vitriol, prison doors slamming in the halls of darkness, judges' gavels falling in contempt, automobile engines racing, hypocrites clamoring for higher profits, and heretics worshiping a false-god called "Mother Earth." We have chosen the fireworks of the battlefield over mending our broken peace, brute force over logical understanding, discord instead of social unity, and the compromise of our Christian convictions in the face of rampant assaults against the Truth. Should we not, instead, be hewing to the same holy invocations and requisitions before God for the healing of our lands? There has been too much world-warring between allies and axises, crafting against the witch-world, planning in the night for the uncertain future, vindictiveness over vindication—not knowing that the spirit of Sir Winston Churchill is hiding in the wings asking us to revel the virtues of faith, hope, and charity over the forensics of blood, sweat, and tears. If we allow our hearts to be infiltrated by the power of the Holy Spirit through the intercession of the Blessed Virgin Mary, we will see the world from the stars overhead and comprehend the gravity of our misguided goals through the clarity of the angels. Now is the time for us to transform the ice-crystals of hatred that live in our frigid hearts into glistening facets of the diamond-jewel of God's Holy Love. We cannot hide our true identity behind our eloquent speeches, pretentious forewords, or promises we shall never keep, or conceal the hairline fractures in the foundation of our faith with colorful ground-effects, fender-skirts, or decorative underpinning. As contradictory as it may seem, the world is in a state of perpetual motion, but not really a permanent one. Such is the beating of the heart, the echo of our memories, the liquidity of our assets, the frivolity of our sentiments, and the fragile nature of today's modern genius. The epitaph on the careers of millions of Americans will probably say, "Ignored the Wisdom of the Mother of God," as they join the ranks of contemporary losers who have always called for revenge over forgiveness, pride above modesty, indolence instead of service, and hatred rather than Love. Do we not see the world as a platform that is not unlike a stage composed of wooden planks upon which the arena is brought to life by lights and sounds, the scenery, musical scores, the plot, the climax, and the casts of people who come-out to play? When our dramas, tragedies, comedies, and parodies begin to unfold, do they not seem like a part of Creation where our dreams are finally fulfilled, problems resolved, hidden talents released, distinctions exposed, and tears ultimately shed? No one should believe for a moment that such art is any substitute for true life, but the fulcrum of all human existence should be a product of our capacity to discern the pathogenic from the wholesome and the artifice of physical infatuation from the recognizable authenticity of Divine Love—not in the sense that our minds should take control of our hearts or that we should erect a sincerity-tester around the circumference of the world; but that our unity under the oath of Christianity must be our hope for the restoration of an international faith and a shared Communion on a globe where neither one seems too welcome these days. Miracles do occur when we allow God to try His best toward bringing His supernatural graces before the ordinary world; certainly not the least of which is the intercession of His Immaculate Mother, the Virgin Mary, the Handmaiden of the Annunciation who gave birth to His Incarnate Son.

There is a vast difference between a daydream and an illusion, a nightmare and the horrors of waking life, and the inspiring compared to the mundane. Our Lady has come to tell us that the world is upside down right now, and we do not yet realize that Jesus is going to return someday soon and invert it with everything He has revealed through His first Apostles, the Saints, every syllable of the Holy Scriptures, and the gift of His Mother's miraculous messages in places like Fatima, Lourdes, Guadalupe, and at the Vatican, itself. It is very difficult for us to know that we are not seeing reality as it should be because we are required to enlist the power of a faith in which different Christians hold many varying opinions. Some of the distinctions between this world and the next would be more apparent than we realize if we ever brought ourselves to accept the principled power of Catholic Truth. One might say that those who are in tune with Christ see mortal life in the shape of an *8*, knowing that it will be much the same configuration when He arrives again to turn it upside down. We are far too concerned about how ungracefully we are aging nowadays, too, and that our dignity is being somehow stolen from us because we have new aches and pains to bear, back-problems, headaches, less energy, more lethargy, heart and lung diseases, susceptibilities to viral infections, varicose veins, poor eyesight, deteriorating teeth, lack of balance, and slowly graying hair. It seems as though the least thing we worry about is what will happen to our soul when we finally die; but we must never lose sight of the goal of arriving intact in Paradise someday. Our devotion to the Blessed Mother will keep the focus of our vision trained upon that stupendous moment of our mortal passing. Her intercession is our treasure trove of Wisdom in the art of living the fullness of God's grace and peace. In the words of the great Doctor of the Church, Saint Anselm (1033-1109), *"...Blessed Lady, sky and stars, earth and rivers, day and night—everything that is subject to the power or use of man—rejoice that through you they are in some sense restored to their lost beauty and are endowed with inexpressible new grace. All creatures were dead, as it were, useless for men or for the praise of God who made them. The world, contrary to its true destiny, was corrupted and tainted by the acts of men who served idols. Now, all Creation has been restored to life and rejoices that it is controlled and given splendor by men who believe in God. The universe rejoices with new and indefinable loveliness. Not only does it feel the unseen presence of God, Himself, its Creator, it sees Him openly, working and making it holy. These great blessings spring from the Blessed Fruit of Mary's Womb. Through the fullness of the Grace that was given you, dead things rejoice in their freedom, and those in Heaven are glad to be made new. Through the Son who was the glorious Fruit of your Virgin Womb, just souls who died before His life-giving Death rejoice as they are freed from captivity, and the Angels are glad at the restoration of their shattered Domain. Lady, full and overflowing with Grace, all Creation receives new life from your abundance. Virgin, blessed above all creatures, through your blessing, all Creation is blessed, not only Creation from its Creator, but the Creator, Himself, has been blessed by Creation. To Mary, God gave His only begotten Son, whom He loved as Himself. Through Mary, God made Himself a Son; not different, but the same by nature: Son of God and Son of Mary. The whole universe was created by God, and God was born of Mary. God created all things, and Mary gave birth to God. The God who made all things gave Himself form through Mary, and thus, He made His own Creation. He who could create all things from nothing would not remake His ruined Creation without Mary. God, then, is the Father of the created world, and Mary the Mother of the re-created world. God is the Father by whom all things were given life, and Mary the Mother through whom all things were given new life. For God begot the Son, through whom all things were made, and Mary gave birth to Him as the Savior of the world. Without God's Son, nothing could exist; without Mary's Son, nothing could be redeemed. Truly the Lord is with you, to whom the Lord granted that all Nature should owe as much to you as to Himself!"* (Oratio 52: 158, 955-956).

Leaping storm troopers, flying smart-bombs, chemical warfare, and weapons of mass-destruction could never keep the children of Mary from gathering around the firelight of Her Immaculate Heart or from taking shelter beneath Her stately Mantle. Saint Anselm was correct from the very start: all Creation has been given new life because of the compliant *Fiat* and sincere holiness of the Mother of God, who bore Our Savior into the Flesh of Man in the quiet solitude of the night; reared Him with great Love and Wisdom with Saint Joseph in Nazareth, stood beside Him faithfully and sorrowfully beneath the Holy Cross, received His deposed Corpse which lay upon Her lap, rejoiced with Him during His Easter Resurrection, bade Him farewell at His Cardinal Ascension, and has since received *Her* Crown as Queen of Heaven and Earth after Her Glorious Assumption into the Light of Paradise to reside with the Almighty Father, Her Sacrificed Son, the Holy Spirit, the Saints in the realms of Glory, and all the angelic choirs. When we believe this with all our hearts, growing older will not seem to bother us that much anymore because our pains and strife will become an ullage for the Passion and Crucifixion of Jesus Christ; as we are sustained by His promise to rescue us from the grave. *Come, sweet soothing bath of Holy Immortality! Immerse us in Eternal Light! Set us free at last! We shall not fear our dying anymore!* When we are unsure as to whether free and extraordinary men are giving the best of themselves to God, we can always hold them beside the endless loyalty of the Immaculate Conception as a measure of their Love. If our brothers' friendship seems too lukewarm or our neighbors' affinity does not ring so loudly anymore, we can always hear the intonation of the affection of Mary clearly through the elevation of Her prayers and in the piety of Her mortal children, Her entourage of angels, and through the Holy Spirit: the voice of God, Himself. If a gloomy, cold loneliness ever looms across the surface of our days, the blessing of the Lady of Perpetual Help will take us to the Light, for we have recourse in this Woman of Benign Dominion. Let every priest and parishioner turn to Her for assistance in their prayers; for She knows the Sacred Heart of Jesus better than any other soul to have ever lived within the limits of the world. She will summon the Holy Paraclete to protect our innocent children from any further harm and, likewise, guide those who might be tempted to fall into sin from surrendering to their weaknesses. When all is said and done, the sacred gift of Christianity; even with the many factions which are found today therein; will discover that it is Mary who has been shielding us from the Wrathful Justice of an outraged God by forewarning us in advance. All Creation will ultimately ascertain that the fateful course of human events was openly revealed and carefully unfurled according to the willingness of the children of Light to take their Mother's hand.

There is more than just Sacred Tradition that takes us to our knees in honor of the Blessed Virgin Mary because Her role in our Redemption is strewn like a pathway of flowering *phlox* across the acreage of Creation. While Saint Peter is the foundation upon which Christ begot the Church under Himself as the Capstone, His Mother is the central Pillar who has been providing its Holy Grace since the arrival of the blazing flames of Pentecost. What does it mean to say that She was the first sinless Virgin to have ever been conceived? We all know that Eve was born in perfection, but in her collusion with Adam, they abused their will and chose to disobey. Although they were created without sin, they willfully chose to commit a wanton offense against God and, thereby, desecrated the nature of their souls, aligning themselves with outright evil, and choosing the coals of corruption over the pearls of chastity. With this, they manifested their own condemnation. The Blessed Virgin Mary, on the other hand, certainly had a Will, but there was absolutely nothing in Her "being" that would allow Her to conjure the thought of denying God. Her soul is the articulate *enunciation* of the Love of the Almighty Father to whom Her entire life was given on the occasion of the Annunciation of the Angel Gabriel who had come to ask Her to bear the Son of Man in the bounty of Her Womb; and, thereby, She became the Ark of the New Covenant of the Eternal Salvation of the Earth. *"Be it done to Me according to your Word,"* was Her response, giving flight to the constellation of the Magnificat which would eventually become Her Crown of Twelve Stars. Let all humankind understand this clearly—the Will of God-inviolate was present in Mary long before He sent His Spirit to the Earth in the form of a dove and tongues of fire on the Feast of Whitsunday. His sinless Mother already knew Him and was predisposed to complying with His wishes from the moment She was first conceived in the womb of Her mother, Saint Anne. The Salvific Mysteries of the Trinity of God were made complete when Mary said *Yes* to the Archangel that day. The parallel is this: Mary could not deny the request of God any more than Jesus Christ could have told Her that He would come-down from the Cross on Good Friday if She had asked. She did not, however, because She knew the reason She was born was to bear the Messiah for the Redemption of the entire human race. Let us not forget that the caveat of this is that Our Lady was placed into Creation by God so that He, too, could have a Woman to affectionately call His *Mother*. Indeed, He fashioned the entire galaxies and universes around His admiration for Her Grace. The only reason He made flowers to be pretty was so they could imitate Her eyes. The very fragrance of Divine Love is emitted by this Virgin from such an humble origin. She is all comeliness, obedience, and peacefulness in the world, the same way that Her Son is living power and omnipotence. She is the Tree of Life from whom the Fruit of Love, Jesus Christ, bloomed into Creation, and has always been elegant, never shedding Her foliage, as colorful as the autumn and, yet, as forever budding as a towering oak in the spring. Her Mantle is as broad as the skyline overhead, not unlike a greenhouse donned by the globe to preserve the purity of our invisible souls from any elemental harm. Her prayers are our unspoken dreams for happiness, and Her piety the precise archetype of the Love we are supposed to seek.

No interior agony would defy the pleasance of Her virtue; and neither could Her weeping wash-away the beauty of Her Face. She is the Fountain of Christ's forgiving Mercy, His devotion for the blessed, fervency for the faint-of-heart, the constancy of living patience, and our best friend on Judgment Day. The sweet melodies of Saint Elmo's Fire, Amazing Grace, and Edelweiss are concealed inside the stanzas of Her Immaculate Heart, for in this Creature lives the clemency of the breezes in the dog-days of summer, the flourishing of the waters in the barren deserts of our lonely discontent, our shawl of warmth in the bleakness of mid-winter, and the daybreak of our hopes atop the summit of Christ's Love in our dark and painful hours. *Let every nation know that Jesus Christ will never take the Earth back into the Light of Paradise until each and every one of us has been fashioned by the Immaculate Heart of His Mother so that we can become Marian remnants in the likeness of Himself!* Take that!—you Protesting naysayers all! Oh! We dare not express our highest jubilation quite yet in acclamation for this Truth! Let us hold some in reserve because the best is still to come! The climax of our joy in the stature of this Lady has yet to fall from the precepts of God's Paradise! We must be patient, lest we give our Almighty Father cause to relent in His routing of the enemies of His Immaculate Queen! Even the God who gave us life will follow our lead in venerating the Patroness of the Saints because His own loveliness will become absorbed in our devotion to Her Grace! Creation is bulging into a swell in which She has been stationed as the Grand Marshalette! When Her Son finally pulls-out all the stops to conclude mortal time, streamers of our petitions that have been silently waiting in the wings will be released from under Her Veil, the ones we forgot to utter during our bedtime prayers when we were still little children, genuflecting on our knees with our eyes closed as we leaned across our blankets in the hope of rising tomorrow with happiness anew. Mary of the Joyful Nativity is about to lead the Victory parade of the dynamic Love of Jesus Christ over the hatred of the world! She will finally part Her hands that have been folded in holy supplication, and out will fall the Key to our Salvation in the shape of the Cross, finely forged, hewn, and sparked by the friendly-fires of Her Immaculate Heart in which we shall die a willing death to our good fortune and be raised to the reveille of God's Bleeding Son, still being held within the moistened palms of obedience by the Gentle Lady of untold charm. The chevrons on our sleeves will be transformed into the golden boardwalks beneath our feet as we shall join the ranks of those who have been rightly overturned to God through the Bloodshed of His Sacrificed Son. Therefore, let no one speak too soon, ever rush to judgment, or walk-out of the world's theatre-in-the-round before the curtain of the last act of our Creator has been played; for we can already hear one last set of genteel footsteps walking close behind; the Mother of this God who is carefully carrying Her Slain Child in Her bosom like a crystal chandelier the size of Frankfurt am Main! All of our confusion will be gone in the matter of a flash when the veil of our human mortality is lifted and we feel its spell kissing the cheeks of our faces with confetti flying everywhere. This will occur whenever the Mother of God reassures Him that His faithful Church is properly clad in the accorded decency of our hope-inspirited souls.

Soon, and very soon, there will be no more highs and lows, ups or downs, or dims and darks; for only the spires of the summit of ecclesiastical Love will prevail in which we shall see the Light of Truth so profoundly that we will be temporarily blinded once again! Let no one leave the stadium because the Triumph of the Immaculate Heart of Mary is the world, itself, in the bottom of the Ninth, 2000 years are out, the bases are loaded full of Saints, and Jesus Christ is up to bat, holding a wedge in His hands that has been engraved by the Flames of His Sacred Heart with the indelible words, *The Final Resurrection*. All Creation will come to its feet while the Babe of Bethlehem, the Slugger from the Manger, turns and asks His umpire-Father to take a seat with His fans because there will be no more judgments to call; and He will even retire the humble Holy See who has been crouched behind the Altar because *this* one is going nowhere but *out*, afar, and above! And, with the last pitch of the devil to try to take us down, the Crucified Savior of the fallen world will send us flying through Creation once again, so far past danger into the distant beyond that it will bring His own Father to recall that He made the destination of this Grand Slam on the last minute of the twenty-fourth hour of the sixth day, just to round-out the field. He sees this hope leaping inside us like a little child climbing over a fence as though the Earth is a stony Gibralter, rolling-down from the top of Pikes Peak—inevitable, invincible—like a rock! What am I saying here? The present-day attacks against the Roman Catholic Church have awakened the sleeping giant of the destined Truth in us all! We are stirred to react, raised in dander, and determined to set our righteousness on course for running Satan completely off the map. We Catholics have pulled our weapons out of their holsters and our swords from their sheathes in preparation for the ultimate conquest of our secular foes. It will be near to us presently when we shall exchange the potted roses that are sitting alongside the coffins of the reputations of our impugned priests for long-stem champagne glasses in welcoming their dignity back to life again! The resonance we hear in the background is the intergalactic anthem of the Glory of Paradise; and the Cross is the wand with which God has orchestrated the imminent defeat of the adversaries of Love. Jesus Christ is the harmonious Victor in union with God's battle-plan, His Immaculate Mother is the humble Guest of Honor, and the setting is the last day of the world. We sometimes revolve in and out of believing this, but the Virgin Mary will coax us into holding to such thoughts of Truth permanently, prompting us to listen to the Holy Spirit at the center of our hearts saying with just a twinge of sarcastic joy, *"...it's nice to see you staying longer than ten minutes at a time!"* It is thereafter that we will turn to all those self-aggrandizing naturalists and reveal the hand we have been dealt by Jesus Christ in the manner of defeating their opposition to His Mother's intercessory powers, lay our spread of Love on the table of the Earth, look Her non-Catholic adversaries straight in the eyes, and say with confidence and joy, *"...read'em and weep!"*

     While the poetic license and the widely-metaphoric images that are incorporated into the previous paragraph obviously transmit a parable about the approaching end of the mortal ages, the point is firmly made that Our Lady is going to play a vital role in the shaping of that fateful event. How does humanity know what She is saying around the globe today? We need to look no further than Her faithful Child, the Catholic Church, and to Her priests in whom She affords the strictest confidence. One among them is a member of the Company of Saint Paul named Father Stefano Gobbi, who was born on March 22, 1930 in Dongo, Italy. According to his biography, he was praying in the Chapel of the Apparitions at Fatima, Portugal one day when the Blessed Virgin Mary "impressed" upon him Her wishes that he found the Marian Movement of Priests, which he did on October 13, 1972, precisely 55 years after the supernatural miracle during which 70,000 people saw the sun spinning out of control at Fatima, appear to leave its orbit and descend near the surface of the Earth, parching the ground which had only moments earlier been drenched by torrents of rain. The Holy Mother has spoken to Father Gobbi by interior locution thereafter, giving specific messages to Her priests and the larger family of humanity from 1973 until 1998, a period of a quarter-century. We understand that his messages are now directed for his own spiritual nourishment and sustainment. But, in the span of that twenty-five years, the Mother of God explicated an almost inconceivable manifest of miraculous Truth about the role of Christianity in submitting the world back into the hands of God. While my intention is not to convey messages that have already been spread quite profoundly by the Marian Movement of Priests, I do wish to address the point about the purification of the Catholic Church which has been under discussion since the publication of the weaknesses of some of its clergy. For informational purposes, the United States headquarters of the MMP is located in Saint Francis, Maine, and its National Director for many years, the Reverend Father Albert G. Roux, has written quite extensively about the role of the Immaculate Conception and Her Marian Movement of Priests in cultivating and preparing humanity for the Second Coming of Jesus Christ. I believe it to be rather prescient, relevant, and significant that Father Roux wrote in a Memorandum dated February 22, 2001, the Liturgical Feast of the Chair of St. Peter, about the purification of the Church because it allows us to see its present difficulties with greater perspective than before. Said Father Roux in his revealing monograph, *"...Jesus uses the Church which He has founded as a means to extend His Mercy, His forgiveness, and His graces. The Church, like her Founder, is composed of two natures: human and Divine. Its Divine nature will never be destroyed; the gates of Hell will never prevail against it, much the same as the divinity of Jesus was left unscathed in the aftermath of His Passion and Death. The human nature of the Church, however, has become infected by our sinfulness... The impurities must be purged, and that part of the Church's human element which is corrupt must die before it can once again become more resplendent than ever... The process of dying naturally brings about suffering, and once again, these sufferings will be used by the Holy Spirit to sanctify and purify the Church and its human nature, whereas Satan will use them to try to destroy people's faith. In the end, when all this evil will have been purged, Jesus will renew the Church and will raise it to its glorious state. The Scriptures describe this as the 'New Jerusalem coming down from Heaven, beautiful as a bride,'(cf. Rev. 21:2) 'without spot or wrinkle.' (Eph. 21:27). But first, the Church must die in its human nature in imitation of Jesus, only to be in the end raised, renewed, and sanctified."* (pp. 10-11).

The Holy See of the Roman Catholic Church has yet to render an official declaration concerning Father Gobbi's messages, but it is very obvious that the Marian Movement of Priests, itself, is to be commended for spreading the Gospel of Jesus Christ worldwide, conducting scores of cenacles in nations around the globe, recalling lost souls to the Sacraments of the Church, unifying its priestly vocations under the protection of the Blessed Virgin, and renewing the faith and hope of millions of pilgrims in the work of Jesus to convert His people to His Blood by which we are all redeemed. I realize that there are countless missions and apostolates which are hidden almost secretly on the international continents in these modern times, but surely none of them is of greater importance than the Marian Movement of Priests in expressing the wishful intercession of the Mother of God in transforming the very humanity She was given as Her children by Christ while She stood under the Cross on which He died on the afternoon of Good Friday. It is always wise to rely upon the Wisdom of the Holy Spirit for discernment regarding matters of the future, our spiritual faith, prophetical revelations, and the virtuosity we need to strengthen our Love. If we are to become victors in Christ the way Our Lady has foretold, are we not being called hereby to accede to the motivations and sacrifices that will take us to the summit of Her Holy Presence in the very Kingdom where Her Son is awaiting God's command to enter the Earth in Glory for the final time? Do our hearts not hunger and thirst for the satisfaction of knowing that our labors in Him are never in vain, that the way we live is in direct proportion to the Eternity we shall all inherit, and that those who oppose Jesus must be converted by our Christian Love so they will have no sustainable objection before the Throne of God someday? Our Blessed Mother's plea is for us to project our inward holiness into the outward world so all humanity can see our Love for Christ in tangible ways, making peace in our homes, within our families, and among the sovereign states in the Arabic world where there has been so much desecration and in-fighting at the sites where the life's teachings, the Passion, and the capital Sacrifice of the Man-God ultimately occurred. As I have affirmed in various places in the text of this book, nothing in the secular world can bring us to such faith in Divine Love because its imitation of true goodness is only by accident; its desires for peace are only sporadic; and its fellows would sell the Savior of the World for the cost of a piece of paper if they could use it to inscribe their hatred for Christianity with the stain of their rejection. It would be wholly proper to quote the Blessed Virgin Mary's words to the Marian Movement of Priests through Father Gobbi when Her messages first began, taken from the anthological record, *To the Priests, Our Lady's Beloved Sons*, 15th English Edition, dated June 1994.

"Look at neither the newspapers nor television;
remain ever close to My Heart in prayer.
Nothing else should be of interest or importance
to you, save living with Me, and for Me."

July 8, 1973

"My beloved sons, look with My eyes and you will
see how the Church is being renewed interiorly,
under the powerful action of the Spirit of God...
She is now living through the most painful moments
of her purification. Assisted and comforted by her Mother,
the Church is now climbing the arduous road to Calvary,
where she must again be crucified and immolated
for the good of many of My children."

August 5, 1978

While I would never presume to own the slightest insight about the private conversations that have been conducted and are ongoing between Father Stefano Gobbi and the Mother of God, I would expect that Her messages are as timeless as the Love of Her Resurrected Son. Therefore, when she first admonished the Marian Movement of Priests to refrain from becoming absorbed in the newspapers and television back in 1973, was She not also telling the entire world that the sublime purposes of God are as urgent in the 21st century wherein we see how editors and TV executives are making an absolute sideshow and travesty of the unfortunate sins of a few of our clergy? When we turn-on the cable news networks or see such newspaper headlines as "Crisis in the Priesthood" and "The Scandal Engulfing the Catholic Church," are we not reminded of the prophecy of the Mother of God that such gruesome sensationalism has been in the making for the past thirty years? While the media are calling for "divide, conquer, and destroy," the Virgin Mary is asking for forgiveness, unity, and healing. She will see us through this tragedy of our faults; She will assist us in comforting the afflicted, and God will effect the convalescence of us all inside the dignified purity of His Son's Victory over Death. Let there be no confusion about His Will for the children of Light to heed the call of His Mother as She says with surety, *"....the Triumph of My Immaculate Heart has already begun."* (July 4, 1986). If it would not be improper for me to add a brief addendum herein about my own experiences with the Divine intercession of the Queen of Paradise, I have compiled Her messages to me and a life-long friend into a personal diary, *Morning Star Over America*, a volume in which I have detailed our experiences with this same Matriarch of Creation. Upon having sent Her messages to Father Albert G. Roux, Director of the Marian Movement of Priests, he returned a handwritten letter in which he stated in part, *"...Our Blessed Mother is in a hurry to have us all come back to Her Son. Time is pressing. It seems that we are so slow in responding to Her urgent requests...May persecution never discourage you from doing Our Lady's work."* (April 24, 1991).

While I sincerely appreciate such an inspiring commendation, I also realize what it is like when somebody tries to alter the ugly face of sinful humanity in a world that yields to change only through great agony and resistance; perhaps because it is difficult for them to believe that the God they most often perceive as being so elusive would take time to show His Love in such spectacular ways. The sheerly overwhelming qualities of such Divine revelations as Marian apparitions do not detract from our reasons to have greater faith; indeed, they embolden every desire we might ever have for strengthening it. We should never see it as being counter-intuitive to assume that another miracle might occur at any given moment in time, despite the fact that our enemies on the outside and within the Church still attempt to run roughshod over the dignity of our trust in the Will of God to do whatever He pleases with the Creation He has made. What does this mean for Roman Catholics, our priests, and for the future? How are we, the Mystical Body of Christ, supposed to react to the so-called purification of the Church? There surely must be some inherent factor in the tenets of our faith which corresponds with our awareness that the end of the world will bring wholly different manifestations than any heretofore seen by a mortal man. There still exists the need for societies everywhere to remember the great service the Catholic Church has provided for the past two-thousand years. While our contemporary investigative reporters are looking for the slightest breach in our integrity, they would rather drink poison than dig into the files to see just how many millions of marriages are performed by our priests every year; or the number of adult baptisms, the Christening of our newborn children, the untold amount of Christian burial Masses that are offered; the blessing of homes, articles, and pets; the counseling of wayward teens and estranged couples, educating millions of our students in parochial settings to prepare them for high school and college; feeding, clothing, and housing the poor; traveling to devastated foreign countries to tend to the sick and comfort the dying; and taking the Good News of the Salvation of humankind in the Cross of Jesus Christ to all four corners of the globe. The Church is immeasurably larger than any of its dissenters, more stable than any public institution, prepared for the future in ways not known to any faithless people to have ever walked the face of the Earth, and savvy enough to withstand crass criticism from anyone who would try to effect the elimination or slow undoing of its sacred traditions. Our priests have done more to improve the lot of the poor in the past thirty days in America alone than secularists have offered during the entire history of the larger world combined—politicians, the multi-media, self-serving survivalists, New Age philosophers, state-sponsored think tanks, and especially those faces we see on television every night engaging in their mantra of capitalist propaganda, competing for a higher percentage of viewer-shares. They surely must not know what they are doing because there is no true Manna from Heaven or Bread of Life outside the Catholic Church and those Orthodox Christians recognized by the Supreme Pontiff in Rome; no Sacramental Host is valid anywhere else, and not a single other institution can lay claim to canonizing or invoking the intercession of the Saints who are already living in eternal bliss inside the mansions of Paradise.

Our towering Catholic cathedrals and basilicas are the pinnacles of the grace of God on Earth; glorious, paramount, elegant, commissioned, ordained, chosen, and preeminent. No blue-blooded patriot, ostentatious populist, ruddy tyrant, or celebrated atheist will ever succeed in bringing it down, diminishing its Light, encroaching upon its beauty, or taking-away the original Truth that is vested in the Catechism as its spirited manifest of Apostolic Christianity. A single Pope of the Catholic Church holds more grasp on God's vision for human Salvation with the Staff in his hands than the entire secular world has ever been able to decipher since Adam and Eve were cast-down from the Garden of Eden. All of this has been the design of God by the power of the Holy Spirit through the Divine Motherhood of the Blessed Virgin Mary. She is the watchful protector of His faithful flock, the Morning Star beyond the night, and the hope for millions of poor souls on Earth and suffering in Purgatory who have pined to know their Savior better. She is the Honor who has made the Christ-Child honorable because God, Himself, created Her to be the Handmaid in whom His entire human growth and development would be forthrightly grown. Indeed, the flood of Wisdom into the mortal world was wrought through Her birthing Love for God's Messianic Son; allowing every Christian vessel to rise again in the tide of His dignity, victory, humility, and everlasting peace. And, to this day, when humankind calls-out for Love to their God and Maker, the voice of His holy Will can be heard through the pleading of His Mother to a lost humanity that is still wandering almost aimlessly in the darkness of our vast transgressions.

If we would only listen with the slightest offerance of subtle intensity, we could detect the King of Creation speaking in unison with Her words, *I AM* is here. So, let not our little children be so afraid anymore, and let our Catholic priests uphold their sacred oath by complying with Christ's commands of purity, chastity, charity, and nobleness. Through the help of Immaculate Mary of Bethlehem, we must turn again to God as one people in Jesus; trusting our clergy to guide us back to Him, to strengthen our resolve to be forever pure, giving us the consolation of the Holy Spirit, blessing us in His Name; and most of all, loving us to their deaths.

Conclusion
Have Mercy on Us, O Lord

When the horrible events of September 11, 2001 occurred, it seemed as though Americans everywhere gained a renewed appreciation for the gift of human life; we looked toward our own families with greater Love, and we perceived our nationality through a more pastoral setting than we have, perhaps, since the cessation of World War II. Everyone pledged to help our country rise from beneath the rubble of defeat like a phoenix, taking our dignity and pride back into the skies of our good-old western penchant for survival. Even though our enemies' terrorist violence may never surpass that pyrotechnic flash of hellish rebellion, we must still defeat them to keep the spirit of democracy alive. And, there is no difference in the way we are supposed to remain committed to unity inside the Church and the economy of human Salvation in the Cross of Christianity. Those who foment hatred, brashness, and segregation among us do not share this idealistic goal even though, when all is said and done, no single one of us is going to be held culpable for the errancy of the human race in its current state of disrepair. We fail because of influences of the flesh, but we are raised again by virtue of the influx of Divine revelation upon our spirits. In this, Bishop Fulton Sheen was right on the mark, as usual. He recognized the reciprocal nature of our faith in God and how it affects both the present and the future. If we teach our children to do good things, will we not thereafter heed our own voices by practicing what we preach, desirous of procuring their trust by our good example? There is evidence aplenty which proves us to be a more reflective society than we appear to have become. Indeed, the genesis and derivation of our romance is a function of our disciplined evaluation of the world around us and our capacity to perceive others through the charitable view of ourselves, while also taking into account every facet of our personal mortification for the elevation of moral righteousness, which is often a tick higher than we care to endure. It is possible to build the finer distinctions of our characters upon an intellectual recognition of the existence of God, but history has taught us over and again that it cannot be accomplished without tapping the providence of the human heart. The unique brevity of life ought to teach us that we are not all that adept at determining what our clearer courses of nobility may be; and this is a subject which authors and analysts of all shades have been trying to differentiate for many thousands of years. They tell us that written laws and prominent kings cannot calm the beast groaning inside us because, as ironic as it sounds, it is too savage to respond to anything less than invincible Love. Our predecessors in the United States have been bantering and bickering back and forth for well-over two centuries now, leveraging their wit and trading wares in an effort to discover what it is that evokes such greatness from men. We have grown philanthropists, presidents, ambassadors, professors, and theologians from all walks of life here in our land, but none of them could have sensed within their vision that humane essence which became their understanding of the meaning of life, shared through their faith in a sovereign God.

Jesus Christ seems to be more interested in conducting private conversations with His anonymous little peons sitting in their backyard gazebos in the midwestern countryside than He does the businessmen who walk down Park Avenue in New York City wearing three-piece suits. And, this same Christological simplicity is what is missing from the fabric of America today. What does this say about the witch-hunting that is ongoing against our Catholic clergy?—that we are much too quick to judge an entire sector of people by what the weakest of their ranks might do, and that we live in a century that says, *kill, lest you be killed.* If our TV networks really wanted to contribute something beneficial to our modern democracy, why don't they take their cameras and microphones into the backwoods districts where people sell sweet corn off the back of their trucks, eat hot grits and hominy before going into the timbers to work, hunt possum for supper, and recite the Holy Rosary under shades trees at night? It is a terrible Truth that the visual pictures they are panning to us now are scenes taken mostly out-of-context, sordid in substance, and too skewed to provide an accurate accounting of the way life really is. There is nothing corrupt in our nation, families, businesses, or our Church parishes that cannot be purified by old-fashioned Love. We need to start giving again, wagering less, supporting rather than contending, and sharing instead of compiling. Our spirits need to be rescued from the speedy autobahns of existence and taken back to the proverbial horse-drawn sleigh being pulled down a snowy lane somewhere on a sunny afternoon in the winter. If we cannot do these things well; if we refuse to emancipate one another for everything villainous we have ever done, then the spirit of America is as dead as Abraham Lincoln, himself. Our mortality is our transference into the prescience of Divine perpetuity; and spreading the Holy Gospel is more than just generating a new body of believers because it has eternal consequences for the participants involved. There is sufficient room to walk upon the Earth without stepping on other people's toes; we should consume no more than our allotted portion, make the work of our hands a labor of supernatural Love, and pray together like men-of-war that Jesus Christ will come into His Kingdom once again and redeem us very soon.

Appendix

Consecration to the Immaculate Heart of Mary and The Sacred Heart of Jesus Christ

"I, a faithless sinner, do renew and ratify today into Thy hands, O' Immaculate Mother, the vows of my Baptism, I renounce forever Satan, his pomps and works; and I give myself entirely to Jesus Christ, the Incarnate Wisdom, to carry my cross after Him all the days of my life, and to be more faithful to Him than I have ever been before. In the presence of all the Heavenly Court, I choose you this day for My Mother and Mistress. I deliver and consecrate to you my body and soul, my goods, both interior and exterior, and even the value of all my good actions, past, present, and future; leaving to Thee the entire and full right of disposing of me, and all that belongs to me, without exception, according to Thy good pleasure, for the greater Glory of God, in time and in Eternity. Amen"

-St. Louis de Montfort

"Jesus, we know that you are merciful, and that you have offered your Sacred Heart for us. It is crowned with Thorns and with our sins. We know that you implore us constantly, so that we do not go astray. Jesus, remember us when we are in sin. By means of your Heart, make all men Love one another. Make hatred disappear from amongst men. Show us your Love. We all Love you and want you to protect us with your Shepherd's Heart, and free us from every sin. Jesus, enter into every heart! Knock, Knock at the door of our hearts! Be patient and never desist! We are still closed because we have not understood your Love. Knock continuously! O' Good Jesus, make us open our hearts to you, at least in the moment we remember your Passion suffered for us. Amen."

Dictated by Our Lady to Jelena Vasilj
Medjugorje, Yugoslavia
November 28, 1983

Prayer of the Angel at Fatima

"My God, I believe, I adore, I hope, and I Love Thee! I beg pardon for all those who do not believe, do not adore, do not hope, and do not Love Thee. O' Most Holy Trinity—Father, Son, and Holy Spirit, I adore Thee profoundly, and I offer Thee the Most Precious Body, Blood, Soul, and Divinity of Jesus Christ, present in all the tabernacles of the world, in reparation for all the outrages, sacrileges, and indifference by which He is offended. By the infinite merits of the Sacred Heart of Jesus and the Immaculate Heart of Mary, I beg the conversion of poor sinners."

Prayer to the Mother of Goodness, Love, and Mercy

"O' Mother mine, Mother of goodness, Love, and Mercy, I Love you infinitely and I offer myself to you. By means of your goodness, your Love, and your Grace, save me. I desire to be yours and desire you to protect me. From the depths of my heart, I pray you, Mother of goodness, let me gain Heaven by means of it. I pray you, by your infinite Love, to give me the Grace so that I may love everyone as you have loved Jesus. I pray you to give me the Grace to be merciful towards them. I offer myself to you completely and desire that you will follow my every step because you are full of Grace. And, I desire that I shall never forget this. If, by chance, I should lose your Grace, I pray you to restore it once again."

Prayer to Saint Michael

"Saint Michael, the Archangel, defend us in battle; be our protection against the wickedness and snares of the devil. May God rebuke him, we humbly pray; and do Thou, O' Prince of the Heavenly Host, by the power of God, cast into Hell Satan and all the evil spirits which wander the world seeking the ruin of souls. Amen."